A Princess of Kensington

A Princess of Kensington

Edward German and Basil Hood

MINT EDITIONS

A Princess of Kensington was first published in 1903.

This edition published by Mint Editions 2021.

ISBN 9781513281407 | E-ISBN 9781513286426

Published by Mint Editions®

MINT EDITIONS

minteditionbooks.com

Publishing Director: Jennifer Newens
Design & Production: Rachel Lopez Metzger
Project Manager: Micaela Clark
Typesetting: Westchester Publishing Services

"'*Twas then the green-robed nymph, fair Kenna, came*
(Kenna! That gave the neighb'ring town its name)."

Characters

Sir James Jellicoe (*a Rich Banker*)
Brook Green (*his Junior Clerk*)
Puck (*the Imp of Mischief*)
William Jelf }
Bill Blake }
Will Weatherly } (*Sailors from H.M.S. "Albion"*)
Jem Johnson }
Yapp (*a Policeman*)
Mr. Reddish (*Proprietor of "The Jolly Tar," Winklemouth*)
Old Ben }
James Doubleday } (*Fishermen*)
Recruiting Sergeant (*Royal Marines*)
Oberon (*King of Fairies*)
Azuriel (*a Mountain Spirit*)
Zepherus (*a fairy*)
Joy (*Sir James Jellicoe's Daughter*)
Nell Reddish (*Mr. Reddish's Niece*)
Titania (*Queen of Fairies*)
Butterfly
Dragonfly
Peaseblossom
Cobweb
Moth
Mustardseed
Lady Jellicoe (*wife of Sir James*)
Kenna (*Oberon's Daughter*)
Chorus of Fairies

Act I.—Kensington Gardens—Morning
Act II.—Winklemouth-on-Sea—Afternoon
Period.—The Present Day.

Act I

SCENE.—*Kensington Gardens, near "The Basin."*
TIME.—*The present (1903). It is Midsummer Day, early morning.*
PEASEBLOSSOM *and a few other Fairies discovered.*

SOLO.—PEASEBLOSSOM.

Come, Fairies!
From the East and the West,
From the South and the North,
At Oberon's summons
Come, Fairies! Come forth!
CHORUS (*heard off*): We come!
PEASEBLOSSOM: Come, Fairies!
To the Court of King Oberon!
Come, Fairies!
To the Gardens of Kensington!
CHORUS (*of Girls*): We come! (*Enter Fairies*)
CHORUS: 'Tis Midsummer Day
When every Fay
Doth make a meeting
To give a greeting:
We bid good-day
And then away
Hither, thither,
Everywhither,
To where we dwell
In leafy dell
Or rocky grotto
And this our motto—
"Over hill, over dale,
Thorough bush, thorough briar,
Over park, over pale,
Thorough flood, thorough fire!"
(AZURIEL *enters*)
A FAIRY: Welcome, Azuriel!
AZURIEL: Say, rather, ill-come; since I come with care;

Sour Melancholy reigning in my heart,
Like Hecate in Hades!

BUTTERFLY: Why Melancholy, Spirit?

AZURIEL: Spirit, why
Does Night-time follow Day, or Jealousy
Run yelping at the dancing heels of Love?

BUTTERFLY: I know not. A swallow once snapped at my heels,
thinking they were butterflies; and I led them a pretty dance,
thus—(*demonstrates*)

A FAIRY: Hail, Kenna! Daughter of King Oberon!

A FAIRY: Hail, Kenna! Princess of Kensington!

ALL: Hail, Kenna!

Enter KENNA.

AZURIEL: Why come you?

KENNA: I know a Cloud
Who fell in tears of rain!
By Oberon endow'd
With beauty, she was vain;
Oh, pray she be allow'd
To climb to heaven again!

AZURIEL: Go to thy mortal lover!

KENNA: Love immortal
Bade me come hither to Azuriel!

AZURIEL: Now hither comes thy father, Oberon,
To hold Midsummer Court. Pray him to judge
'Twixt me and thee.

KENNA: So be it. I'll abide
Thy bride or not, as Oberon decide.

CHORUS (*Enter Male fairies*): From where the Scotch mountains,
In mantles of grey,
Stand staring at England
Like chieftains at bay.
Or showing the tartan
In which they're array'd—
Where the purple of heather
Meets green of the glade:
From where the sweet fountains
Down Devonshire way
Run laughing and tumbling

Like children at play,
Or aspen-leaves tremble
From sunshine to shade
Like the thoughts of a lover
Who doubteth his maid:
We have flown through the moonbeams,
Unseen and unknown,
Like the shadows of kisses
A maiden hath blown!

A FAIRY (*spoken*): Hail, Oberon!

ALL: Hail, Oberon! Hail Titania!

Enter OBERON *and* TITANIA, *with* COBWEB, MOTH, *and*
MUSTARDSEED.

DUET.—OBERON *and* TITANIA.

OBERON: Mortal King may ride a-horseback,
    Lords and ladies in his train:
    I do ride upon a swallow
    Bridled with a silken rein!
    Who will follow, follow, follow,
    Who will follow in my train?

THREE FAIRIES: We do follow, follow, follow—
    Cobweb, Moth, and Mustardseed!
    Thorough bush and thorough briar,
    Over hill and over dale!
    Thorough flood and thorough fire,
    Over park and over pale!

TITANIA: Mortal Queen may dance in ball-room
    Under glaring chandelier:
    I do choose a moss-grown hollow
    When the moonlight doth appear!
    Who will follow, follow, follow,
    When the dance I lead?

THREE FAIRIES: We do follow, follow, follow—
    Cobweb, Moth, and Mustardseed!

ALL: We will follow, follow, follow,
    Cobweb, Moth, and Mustardseed!

(*Dance*)

TITANIA: A thousand years have blossomed, faded, died,
    And bloomed again since we saw Kensington.
OBERON: 'Twas here, a thousand years ago, I held
    My fairy court. Our daughter Kenna gave
    Her name to Kensington: and Kensington
    Gave Kenna many beauties in return.
    Sunshine of Kensington gave Kenna hair;
    Blue sky of Kensington gave Kenna eyes;
    Roses of Kensington her cheeks and lips;
    Saplings her shape, and singing birds her voice!
    In gracious Kenna, such as mortal eyes
    Had never seen, until Prince Albion
    Beheld them all in Kenna—and beholding,
    Loved her.
KENNA: But Kenna loved Azuriel.
AZURIEL: And what of Albion?
KENNA: I pitied him.
AZURIEL: And pity claims first-cousinship with love.
KENNA: Which love denies. 'Twas Puck who prompted me
    To do the deed I gladly would undo!
OBERON: Come, mischief-making Puck! I summon you!
BUTTERFLY (startled): Oh! oh!
TITANIA: What is it, Butterfly?
BUTTERFLY: A mouse ran over my foot!
GIRLS: A mouse!
OBERON: 'Tis Puck, I warrant. He will come in any shape rather than
    his own. Hunt him! Ho, a mouse! A Puck! A cloak, some one, and
    cover him! (They hunt the mouse, and one throws a cloak over it)
A FAIRY: He is here.
OBERON: Come, Puck! 'Tis Oberon who summons you!
(PUCK rises under the cloak)
PUCK: I am Puck, the Imp of Mischief!
    Of my talents mischief is chief!
    I can plague and irritate you.
    Bother and exasperate you,
    In a manner so perplexing,
    Job himself would find it vexing!
    If a bishop I should fix on
    As a peg to hand my tricks on,

I'm prepared to bet him level
He will wish me where he shouldn't!

OBERON: Now, Mischief! leave folly, and come to the matter
in hand.

PUCK: Here is the matter in a nutshell. (*He produces a nut from
which he takes a document*) And to suit the subject, which is a
lover's quarrel, the parchment is made of mooncalf skin, the
pen was a goose-quill, and the ink a snake's venom. Butterfly,
my valise! As this is a Court of Law as well as a Court of Love,
I'll wear wig and gown, which were invented by the first lawyer:
the one to cover his horns and the other his tail. So! Whereas,
howbeit, hereinafter, and because one thousand years ago
Kenna, Princess of Kensington, being in mortal shape, the
mortal Prince Albion fell in love with her, being wise, abut the
immortal Azuriel had already done the like, being likewise.
Is that true?

KENNA: 'Tis true enough.

PUCK: But not enough truth, seeing there's more to tell.

OBERON: We'll hear it all.

PUCK (*to* KENNA): Do you deny that Albion pray'd
To Neptune for the Sea-God's aid,
That he would help him to elope
With you? A thousand years ago?

KENNA: 'Tis true!

PUCK: Do you deny that Neptune sent
A yellow fog with this intent,
A London fog of sulphur smoke
To serve Prince Albion as a cloak
While he was trying to elope
With you? A thousand years ago?

KENNA: 'Tis true!

PUCK: Do you deny it drove *us* forth
To East and West and South and North;
But through a well-deserved mishap
Was Albion caught in his own trap,
For he contracted such a cough
That he himself was carried off
While he was trying to elope
With you? A thousand years ago?

KENNA: 'Tis true!

PUCK: Do you deny that making use
    Of magic dandelion juice
    You brought his body back to life.
    Although you were the promised wife
    Of him we call Azuriel;
    And by a magic fairy spell
    You changed his death into a sleep
    Extremely long and very deep,
    A sleep that was designed to last
    A thousand years—which now have passed—
    So he is somewhere safe and sound
    (Above or underneath the ground)—

KENNA: 'Tis true!

PUCK: There is the matter in a nutshell; which, as it is a matter of a thousand years ago, might be well chosen a chestnut.

AZURIEL: The matter is a matter of to-day.
    Listen! Find Albion, who's now alive,
    And, as I'll wager, now in Kensington;
    Find Albion, and show him to me married
    By set of sun unto some mortal maid,
    And with the sun shall sink my jealousy
    Of Kenna, and my dark distrust of her. (*Exit*)

OBERON: So be it. Help her, Puck. Find Albion;
    And, having found him, find for him a wife,
    And so shall end these lovers' loveless strife.

TITANIA: We will away! Come, spirits!

PUCK: Stay! I pray you not to go far, but be ready to return; and in mortal attire as well as mortal shape.

OBERON: Why?

PUCK: Because to find a certain man and an uncertain woman and make them marry by sunset is a difficult song to sing solo. I would have a chorus to share the burden of it.

OBERON: So be it. Instruct them as you will. (*to* TITANIA) Come! (*Exeunt*)

PUCK: The lesson is easily learned; that among mortals, where I am to go at your bidding, he goes furthest who has the biggest following.

Song and Chorus.—Puck.

PUCK: If we pass beyond the portals
    That divide us from the mortals,
    You will come upon the custom of the "claque,"
    And the duties of a chorus
    Will be constantly before us—
    The advantage of a chorus at your back.

    A private little chorus at your back,
    A friendly little chorus at your back,
    And the British people, bless 'em,
    You'll be certain to impress 'em,
    If you travel with a chorus at your back!
CHORUS: A private little chorus etc.
PUCK: In a world of advertising
    It is not at all surprising
    That a man who's not a gull should be a quack!
    But you need not be so blatant
    In the pushing of a patent
    If you utilize a chorus at your back!

    That friendly little chorus at your back,
    The chorus of approval at your back,
    You should buy a drum and thump it,
    But let others blow your trumpet—
    That's the duty of the chorus at your back.
CHORUS: That friendly little chorus etc.
(*this verse does not appear in the vocal score*)
PUCK: Now a leading Politician
    In a prominent position
    Is particularly open to attack.
    And he'll find it reassuring
    When he wants to go a-touring
    To travel with a chorus at his back!

    A chorus of approval at his back!
    The chorus of his Country at his back!
    He'll be looking through a spy-glass

Or a telescope or eye-glass
At the chorus that awaits his coming back!

CHORUS: A chorus of approval etc.

Exeunt all but PUCK *and* KENNA.

KENNA: Puck! Now my happiness hangs on three threads: to find
Albion, to find he has forgotten me, and to find a maid he'll marry.

PUCK: By sunset! That's the finding of the Court—and I wish they'd
done their own finding.

KENNA: How shall we find Albion?

PUCK: Dead as a dried herring. As he has been since a thousand years.

KENNA: Since *when*?

PUCK: Since he died.

KENNA: But since he did *not* die—

PUCK: He died well enough—for a man who had no previous
experience.

KENNA: But the spell you taught me to pronounce?

PUCK: Might have been mispronounced, for all the good it could do.

KENNA: If this be true, why did you not tell it to Azuriel?

PUCK: Because there are three things that waste time in the telling:
wisdom to a fool, folly to a wise man, and the truth to a jealous lover.

KENNA: That is true. He would not believe the truth now. He believes
Albion is still alove, and nothing will satisfy him but to see him
married. What shall we do if Albion is truly dead?

PUCK: Find a false Albion that your lover will believe the true one.

KENNA: Yes, yes! Some one that Azuriel shall think is Albion, and see
married to some mortal maid by my connivance, and so be satisfied,
and his jealousy die of starvation. See to it, Puck! Good Puck!
Sweet Puck! See to it!

PUCK: Say that again!

KENNA: See to it!

PUCK: No—my name, with sweet added to it, like treacle to suet
pudding.

KENNA: Those who Hobgoblin call you, and sweet Puck,
You do their work and they shall have good luck! There!

PUCK: Now we'll play a puppet-show, in which mortals are the dolls,
and I pull the strings. Butterfly! (*Enter* BUTTERFLY)

BUTTERFLY: Here!

PUCK: Know you Waterloo Station, arrival platform, South Western
Railway.

BUTTERFLY: Yes. Suburban?

PUCK: Main-line. Arriving in a certain train
    You'll find four foolish mortals, dress'd in blue,
    And on their heads are caps, and on the caps
    The name of "Albion" in golden letters.

KENNA: Who are these men?

PUCK: Four sailors from H.M.S. "Albion"
    On leave from Portsmouth. One of them we'll make
    Azuriel believe is Albion,
    Because that name is written on his hat.
    (*To* BUTTERFLY) By the illusion of some fairy trick
    Convey them hither quickly.

BUTTERFLY: Quickly! (*Exit*)

PUCK: Look!
    Here comes another puppet. He's a banker
    Who lives in Palace Gardens, Kensington.
    And he, according to a foolish vow,
    Each day at dawn bathes in the Serpentine.
    I know a bank where he will lay his clothes:
    I, in the small resemblance of a dog,
    Will carry them away when he's undress'd
    And put them on myself; not only them,
    But his appearance too—his outward shape,
    Bald head, grey whiskers, embonpoint and all!
    So his own wife shall think that I am he—
    Await developments, and wait for me!

KENNA: I'll wait! (*Exit*)

PUCK: As "Sir James Jellicoe," anon
    I'll make my daughter marry Albion! (*Exit*)

SIR JAMES JELLICOE *enters. As he crosses the stage* BROOK *enters, running after him.*

BROOK: Sir James! Sir!

JELLICOE: Brook Green? Why are you in Kensington Gardens, and in
    your volunteer uniform?

BROOK: I thought I might meet you on your way to the Serpentine, sir,
    and I want to ask you if I may have a holiday to-day sir.

JELLICOE: A holiday? You had twelve months' holiday last year, to
    enable you to go and fight the Boers.

BROOK: Yes, sir.

JELLICOE: And you want a whole day now?

BROOK: Yes, sir.

JELLICOE: How do you mean to enjoy yourself *this* time?

BROOK: As to-day is the longest day, sir, I thought that after my early morning parade I would like to spend it—. I hardly know how to tell you, sir; but will you glance at this photograph?

JELLICOE (*taking it*): My daughter?

BROOK: Yes, sir.

JELLICOE: And you?

BROOK: Yes, sir.

JELLICOE: What does this mean?

BROOK: It means that we have both made an engagement which we hope very much we may be able to keep.

JELLICOE: Bless me! You wish to marry my daughter—Miss Joy Jellicoe?

BROOK: Yes, sir. I daresay you think it very impertinent of me to wish such a thing—

JELLICOE: I should think it much more impertinent of you *not* to. Any young man might be proud to marry her.

BROOK: Yes, sir.

JELLICOE: Then why shouldn't *you*?

BROOK: I don't know, sir!

JELLICOE: No more do I!

BROOK: Thank you, sir!

JELLICOE: Is there any other subject you wish to thrash out with me?

BROOK: I only wish to say that I regard your daughter as a princess, sir. And as her favourite subject, I am glad you don't want to thrash *me* out! Thank you, sir!

JELLICOE: Thank her, my boy. And—you may take all day thanking her, if you like. (*Exit*)

DUET.—BROOK *and* JOY.

BROOK: Seven o'clock in the morning,
Upon a day in June!
A thousand throats
Do pipe glad notes,
And I will join their tune
And greet my love,
My sweet, my love,

And sing my love a lay,
At seven o'clock in the morning,
Upon a summer's day!

Enter JOY.

JOY: Seven o'clock in the morning,
And I am out betimes,
For who'll be said
To lie abed
And listen to the chimes?
We'll meet, my love,
And greet, my love,
And join the roundelay
All Nature sings in the morning
Upon a summer's day.

BROOK: Joy!

JOY: Yes, dear?

BROOK: I have told your father.

JOY: And I have told mother.

BROOK: What did she say?

JOY: She said, "Bless you!" as if she were not surprised.

BROOK: He said, "Bless *me*!" as if he *was*. But he gave me a holiday, and said I might spend the whole day with you.

JOY: And this is the longest day!

BROOK: And we'll be happy as the day is long. Where shall I take you?

JOY: Take me where I've never been before! Take me in a boat on the Serpentine.

BROOK: One can't go far on the Serpentine.

JOY: *One* can't—but *two* can go as far as Fairyland—if they are the right two.

BROOK: This world is good enough for me. Just now it seems almost too good to be true.

JOY: I wonder if it is—and means to fade away like a cloud castle.

BROOK: No, darling. I don't see anything that can possibly interfere with our happiness.

JOY: Perhaps there are some things we don't see.

BROOK: Well, I don't believe in things I don't see, but I do believe in gipsies—and here comes one. You shall have your fortune told. (KENNA *enters. To* KENNA) I can see you are a gipsy of some sort. I want you to tell this lady's future.

KENNA: Why?

BROOK: Why, because I know it is a happy one. I'll give you a shilling.

JOY: Sixpence is quite enough, dear.

KENNA: I have no use for money.

BROOK: What a curious creature! Show her your hand, dear.

KENNA (*to* JOY): I have no need to look upon your hand,
   For one maid's mind is mirror to them all,
   And gazing in the crystal of my own
   I see your fortune. Listen.

   I know a rose
   That hangs upon a bow'r:
   The sun bade her unclose
   Into a gracious flow'r:
   But sweeter still her sweetness grows
   Beneath a show'r!

   I know a heart—
   It lies within my breast:
   And it hath shown the smart
   Of tears, and Love's unrest:
   But gentle roses tell my heart
   That tears are best!

JOY: She frightens me a little!

BROOK: Nonsense, darling! Nobody believes in gipsies. Come, never mind what she said. *We* shall be all right. (*Exeunt*)

KENNA: All will be well! So roses comfort me,
   In their sweet breath lies sweet philosophy!

Enter AZURIEL.

AZURIEL: Well, how of Albion, Kenna? Is he found?

KENNA: I—I think he will be soon. In brief, shortly. Here's Puck. Ask him.

Enter PUCK, *wearing the appearance of* SIR JAMES JELLICOE.

PUCK: Hail fellow! well met, Azuriel! Know you me?

AZURIEL: Either I mistake your shape and making quite—

PUCK: Yes. I suppose *she* told you, or you'd have never guessed it.
   A woman's tongue is like a dog's tail—best pleased when it is wagging.

EDWARD GERMAN AND BASIL HOOD

AZURIEL: Find Albion, and show him to me married
  By set of sun unto some mortal maid,
  And with the sun shall sink my jealousy
  Of Kenna. Hasten! Find him! I am mad!
PUCK: Then don't be mad here, but justify the proverb, and be out of
  sight, if out of mind. For here comes one woman who'll tale me
  for her husband—and will love me truly, though she be a false wife.
  (KENNA *and* AZURIEL *retire up*)
Enter LADY JELLICOE.
LADY JELLICOE: James! I wanted to meet you; but I didn't think you
  would have finished your swim so soon. Where is your towel, dear?
  You haven't lost it, have you?
PUCK: I left it for *him*. The only covering he has.
LADY JELLICOE: Who's *him*?
PUCK: Hush, my love! Who are *these*?
LADY JELLICOE: Joy and Brook—that's what I wanted to talk to you about.
Enter JOY *and* BROOK.
BROOK: This is the longest day, and we have wasted nearly four hours
  of it. It is past seven, and I have only kissed you once. We have a
  lot of lost time to make up.
JOY: My copy-book used to say, "Lost opportunities are never
  regained."
BROOK: Mine said, "Two heads are better than one." Let's put our two
  heads together—and see if we can't contradict your copy-book.
  (*They do so*)
PUCK: Well, I'm—
LADY JELLICOE: Don't swear, James!
PUCK: Do you know that is my daughter?
LADY JELLICOE: *Our* daughter, dear. You can't expect to find old heads
  on young shoulders.
PUCK: I expect to find my daughter's head on her own shoulders.
LADY JELLICOE: Then you expect too much, dear. Joy—
JOY: Mother!
LADY JELLICOE: Have you told your father?
JOY: Not yet. But Brook has.
PUCK: What did I say?
BROOK: Why, sir, you looked favourably on my suit.
PUCK: Then I believe I have changed.
ALL: Changed!

BROOK: How?

PUCK: In my idea of your suit. It seems to me to be a military suit.
Suppose I prefer a *sailor* suit for my son-in-law?

JOY: What do you mean, father?

PUCK: I mean that you young people must not take your true love as a
matter of course that will run smooth.

LADY JELLICOE: Nonsense, James! Remember how *ours* has been.
There has never been any difference between *us*.

PUCK: There is a great difference between us and *them*.

JOY: Is this what the gipsy meant?

SEXTET.—JOY, KENNA, LADY JELLICOE, BROOK,
PUCK, *and* AZURIEL.

Who that knows how I love you, love,
True love can deny?
Who will say the course of true love

JOY, LADY JELLICOE, BROOK, *and* PUCK: Ever goes awry?   }

KENNA *and* AZURIEL: Never goes awry?   }

ALL: Write him down a fool, fa la!
Send him back to school, fa la!
To learn "Exceptions prove the rule,"
And so do you and I!

Exeunt, PUCK *taking off* JOY.

Enter POLICEMAN YAPP, BILL BLAKE, WILL WEATHERLY, *and* JEM
JOHNSON.

BLAKE: What's this here place, Governor?

YAPP: What's what place?

BLAKE: Why, this here.

YAPP: Kensington Gardens.

BLAKE: What are we doin' in Kensington Gardens?

YAPP: What the juice is the use of askin' *me*?

WEATHERLY: Ask Johnson here—he told the driver where to go.

JOHNSON: It was Jelf as told him—not me! He's a-arguin' with the
cabman now about his fare.

BLAKE: William! (*Calling*)

JELF: Hullo! (*Enters*)

BLAKE: Where did you tell that cabman to go to?

JELF: Where did I tell him to go to? Where do you think?

BLAKE: Was it Kensington Gardens?

JELF: No, it wasn't.

WEATHERLY: Well, that's where he's come to.

JELF: He won't come to for some time yet.

BLAKE: Well, this is a rum start!

JELF (*to* YAPP): Talkin' of rum, where can we get a glass of grog apiece?

YAPP: What do you want with grog at this time o' day?

JELF: What do we want with it? Why to clean our boots with it, of course. You don't suppose we want to *drink* it, do you? Four or'nary sailormen like us! (*Exit* YAPP *taking a note*)

QUARTETTE.—JELF, WEATHERLY, JOHNSON, *and* BLAKE.

ALL: We're four jolly sailormen
  Come up from the sea

JELF: (There's Bill Blake, Will Weatherly,
  Jem Johnson, and me);

ALL: Enjoyin' our liberty
  In fairly good healf—

JELF: (Meanin' Bill Blake, Will Weatherly,
  Jem Johnson, and self).

JELF: We ain't like them Jolly Tars
  You sees in a play,
  A-rescuin' 'eroines
  And shoutin' "Belay!"
  Which them there's burlesquesses
  Of what sailors be
  (Such as Bill Blake, Will Weatherly,
  Jem Johnson, and me).

BLAKE: Our ship ain't no saucy bird
  What "flies o'er the foam,"
  But a darned ugly battle-ship
  What's rolled her way 'ome;
  What's rolled her way 'ome agin
  From the South Chiney sea

BLAKE *and* JELF: (With Bill Blake, Will Weatherly,
  Jem Johnson, and me).

ALL: And maybe we're Handy Men,
  And maybe we ain't;

But this is our characters
Without any paint:
Just four plain bluejackets as
Is rated A.B.

JELF: (Meanin' Bill Blake, Will Weatherly,
Jem Johnson, and me).

HORNPIPE.

Enter PUCK, YAPP, *and a Gardener, the latter bearing a wheelbarrow with various gardening implements.*

PUCK: Good morning, officer!

YAPP: Good morning, Sir James Jellicoe, sir.

PUCK: What have we here? Four fine British sailors, eh? Warm weather, lads!

JELF: Remarkable warm—and dry, sir.

PUCK: What would each of you say to a pint of British beer? What would you say to it, eh?

JELF: We wouldn't stand talkin' to it for long, sir.

PUCK: What are you staring at, officer?

YAPP: I suppose you *are* Sir James Jellicoe, and not his twin brother?

PUCK: I am certainly not my brother. I have no brother, and if I had, I do not think I should be he. Why do you ask?

YAPP: Why, I thought I saw you undressed in the water not two minutes since. And now you're here. It's like a halibi—a halibi in real life! (*Exit*)

PUCK: A great deal can happen in two minutes. In two minutes these fine British seamen may be having a fine British breakfast at my house—a breakfast of British beef and beer—if they will carry this card to 99, Palace Gardens and give it to my butler. What do you say, lads?

JELF: Thank you kindly, sir. (*Exeunt Sailors, singing*)

PUCK (*to* JELF): One moment! (*Detaining him*)

JELF (*calling to others*): Hi!

PUCK: No, let them go. You can't miss the house.

JELF: I may miss the beer, sir.

PUCK: I shall not detain you for a moment. Now, tell me, are you a marrying man?

JELF: No worse than most sailors, sir.

Puck: And you have an eye for female beauty?

Jelf: Two eyes—each like a binocular.

Puck: Then kindly look at this photograph. (*showing photograph*)

Jelf (*whistling*): Was there ever a trimmer, tauter, prettier—

Puck: No, sir, there never was! A photographic camera has answered your question in the negative, of which that is a proof.

Jelf: Well, I'm blest!

Puck: You *shall* be, sir, with a father's blessing! That is my daughter, Miss Joy Jellicoe. You have my permission to fall in love with her.

Jelf: I've done it already, with leave or without! But what about the young man?

Puck: What young man?

Jelf: *Her* young man, I expects. Him that's standin' by her in the picture.

Puck: He will have to be cut out, thus. (*Takes shears from gardener's barrow and cuts photograph, then retains one portion, and hands back the other*) I will see to him. You look after her.

Jelf: I'll show a leg! What did you say her name was?

Puck: Joy.

Jelf (*turning up his sleeves*): I've got a heart somewheres without a name to it. (*Looking at tattoo marks*) Annie—Jane—Sarah—Sophie—here it is. I'll have Bill Blake put an arrer through it, and Mizpah underneath, and give it *her*. He's very good at Mizpah is Bill. There's hardly a man in the ship's company as hasn't two or more of Bill's Mizpahs on him somewheres. (*Exit*)

Puck: Up and down, up and down,
I will lead them up and down;
I am feared in field and town;
Goblin, lead them up and down. (*Exit*)

Enter Ben *and* Doubleday; *enter* Yapp.

Ben: Mister, have you seen such a thing as a sailor—four sailors—about here anywheres?

Yapp: Why?

Ben: Why, us and Mr. Reddish, and Mr. Reddish's niece—

Yapp: Who's Mr. Reddish?

Ben: You don't know Mr. Reddish? Why, Mr. Reddish is the proprietor of an alehouse—that's who Mr. Reddish is.

Yapp: Where?

BEN: Why, at Winklemouth, where we come from—us and Mr. Reddish and Mr. Reddish's niece—to meet William at the Waterloo Station.

YAPP: Who's William?

BEN: Why, my nevvy, William Jelf, as is goin' to marry Mr. Reddish's niece; and we see him jump into a hansom cab with three other sailors afore he has time to see us or us to stop him, and off they goes, and we after, and they're somewhere about, 'cos we come up with their cabman and arst him, and he usin' fearful langwidge about them and all; and that's who William is—one of them four sailors as I'm enquirin' about.

YAPP: What do you want with 'em?

BEN: Why, to know where he is.

YAPP: Well, 'ow should I know? Don't worry about it. I'm in a hurry. (*Exit*)

BEN: Here's Mr. Reddish.

Enter REDDISH.

REDDISH: Have you found William, Ben?

BEN: No, Mr. Reddish, sir—not yet.

REDDISH: There's no need to take your 'at off when you speaks to me now my niece is going to marry your nephew. I've told you that before. Why do you do it?

BEN: I ain't likely to forget the respeck due to the proprietor of a alehouse—if it *'as* been turned into a coffee-shop.

REDDISH: And I ain't likely to forget you if you stand by me in getting rid of the woman as has turned my house upside down. There's no good goin' back, lads. We marries my teetotal niece to William Jelf and settles them down in a coffee-shop of their own at least a hundred miles from Winklemouth.

ALL: Ay, ay!

REDDISH: We marries my niece to William by hook or by crook.

BEN: By 'ook or crook, if a crook or a 'ook can do it.

DOUBLEDAY (*stammering*): What b-b-beats me is, why haven't you t-t-told her to g-go—that's what b-b-beats me.

REDDISH: Oh, that beats you, does it? Well, let me tell you what I tell her she gen'rally contradicts—and what she can't contradict ain't worth mentioning. You're silly, Doubleday; that's what you are, silly.

DOUBLEDAY: W-w-what I m-m-

REDDISH: What *I* mean, and what it means to all of you, is—a pint of ale every night of your lives, with gin in it.

BEN: 'Ush!

Enter NELL.

NELL: What are you talking about, Uncle Reddish?

REDDISH: We was talking about the weather, Nell. (*Winks at* BEN)

NELL: Your heads were remarkably close to be talking about the weather.

REDDISH: It was remarkably close weather we was talking about. You look pale, Nell.

NELL: I have just seen a man with nothing on but a towel.

BEN: Shows 'ow the weather affects some, more than others.

REDDISH: Will you wait here, Nell? We're goin' to see if we can find a public—

BEN: Library—

REDDISH (*aside*): I was going to say that.

BEN (*aside*): You mightn't have thought of it.

REDDISH: We're a-going to see if there's a public library open anywheres. We'll come back and let you know.

NELL: Very well.

REDDISH: You won't go too far by yourself?

NELL: I'm not the sort of girl to go too far with any one.

REDDISH: No. (*Exit all but Nell*)

SONG—NELL.

Oh, what is woman's duty?
It is to use her beauty!
To fill her place
Of gentle grace
In wise Creation's plan!
As sunshine melts the snow
And makes the flowers grow
Doth womankind her grace bestow
Upon disgraceful Man!

Shall woman waster her light on
An Admirable Crichton?
Oh, better far
To be the star
Some wandering soul may scan!
If she her grace bestow

Upon the base and low,
As baking powder is to dough
May woman be to Man!

(*Exit*)

Enter Fairies with OBERON, TITANIA, PEASEBLOSSOM, *and* BUTTERFLY, *all disguised in mortal attire. The girls as Nursemaids, the men as Butchers, Milkmen, Carpenters, Draymen, Sweeps, etc.*

CHORUS.

MEN: We're butchers and bakers
    And candlestick makers,
    And members of every trade!
GIRLS: No doubt you are able
    Our calling to label
    As that of a nursery-maid!
ALL: And nobody guesses
    Because of our dresses
    (Which we have obtained upon hire)
    Oh, no one aware is
    We're all of us Fairies
    Parading in mortal attire!
MEN: But though we doff
    Artistic and poetic coats,
GIRLS: We don't take off
    Our natures with our petticoats!
MEN: And if perchance
    You overrate our densities,
GIRLS: In song and dance
    We'll show you what nonsense it is!

TARANTELLE.—BUTTERFLY.

(*Enter* KENNA)

SONG.—KENNA.

Twin butterflies
That fitfully fall and rise

Are a fairy's feet!
Then lightly spread
A carpet of woven song,
The gossamer bed
Her feet may float along!

Music as gay
As the laugh of a girl at play,
And soft and sweet!
The gossamer thread
That fairies float along,
Oh, lightly spread
A carpet of woven song!

(*Exit*)

TITANIA: Do you think we are sufficiently disguised?

OBERON: To go among men? Why, yes, they will take no notice
of us.

BUTTERFLY: That depends. I mean them to take some notice of *me*.
Here comes one for a beginning. I'll speak to him.

TITANIA: Have a care. I wager he'll suspect you for a spirit.

BUTTERFLY: I'll wager. (BROOK *enters*) (*To* BROOK) Greeting,
friend.

BROOK: Eh?

BUTTERFLY: Now look at me well. Take a good look.

BROOK: You have good looks to spare.

BUTTERFLY: What would you take me for?

BROOK: A sweetheart, perhaps, if I hadn't one already, whom I'm now
looking for.

BUTTERFLY: What manner of man are you?

BROOK: A lover of one girl.

BUTTERFLY: Is that strange in London?

BROOK: Why?

BUTTERFLY: We are. So we question for information. What
are you?

BROOK: A Londoner by birth, a bank clerk by trade, a poor man
by circumstance, a happy one by good fortune, and a lover by
parenthesis.

MILKMAN: Is that all shown by your clothes, as my trade is by
mine?

BROOK: No, my merry milk-merchant. For while I serve the
King with land force, you serve his subjects with watered
weakness.

MILKMAN: I do not understand. I like your clothes better than my
own. What do they mean?

BROOK: Why, that we are a nation of shopkeepers, and this is what's
worn by the boys who mind the shop.

MILKMAN: I would like to be one.

OTHERS: And I, and I, and I.

BROOK: Well, that shows a good spirit. It has been among us
Londoners for a good many centuries. The fighting spirit of the old
London apprentices.

SONG.—BROOK *and* CHORUS.

Now, here's to the 'Prentices
Who lived in Old London
When Hampstead and Highgate
Lay outside the town!
When the wrong and the right of it
Could make a fair fight of it
And no one made light of it
When cudgel met crown!

It was up with your cudgels,
Ye London apprentices!
Up with your cudgels
And lay them not down!
Till good work be well done
And ill work be undone,
By the lads of old London
Who work in the town!

CHORUS: 'Twas up with your cudgels, etc.

BROOK: And whence did the cudgel come?
It sprang from an acorn:
It grew on an oak-tree
Of good green and brown!
English the stock of it,
And hearty the knock of it,

And who would make mock of it
When cudgel came down?

It was up with your cudgels, etc.
CHORUS: 'Twas up with your cudgels, etc.
BROOK: And what of the Londoner
    Who now lives in London?
    Who carries a rifle
    And camps on the Down?
    English the seed of him,
    And London the breed of him—
    When his country has need of him
    He'll fight for the Crown!

    And it's up with your rifles,
    You Volunteer riflemen!
    Up with your rifles,
    And lay them not down!
    Till good work be well done
    And ill work be undone,
    By the lads of old London
    Who trade in the town!
CHORUS: 'Twas up with your rifles, etc.
    (*this verse does not appear in the vocal score*)
    Brook. Then here's to the Riflemen
    Of Town or of Country,
    And here's to his Rifle
    Of Brummagem brown!
    English the stock of it,
    The barrel and lock of it!
    May he who'll make mock of it
    Be shot for a clown!

    When it's "Up with old England,
    And down with her enemies!
    Up with old England,
    For country and crown!"
    May good work be well done
    And ill work be undone

By the lads of old London

Who come from the town!

(*Exit all*)

CHORUS: When it's "Up with old England" etc.

Enter PUCK, *followed by* YAPP.

PUCK: Up and down, up and down—

YAPP: Stop thief! Give me them clothes! Do you hear? Give me them clothes!

PUCK: What clothes?

YAPP: The clothes belongin' to Sir James Jellicoe, the banker, as you came up while he was bathing and took off.

PUCK: Do you mean that *I* took off these clothes?

YAPP: Yes.

PUCK: My dear sir, he took them off himself.

YAPP: I mean you took 'em off while he was in the water.

PUCK: But *he* took them off, before he went into the water!

YAPP: I mean, you took 'em off the bank—

PUCK: Ah! you don't mean I took 'em off the banker?

YAPP: You know what I mean well enough. You took 'em off and put 'em on! You're makin' me giddy. Just you stand still.

PUCK: I prefer to run still. Ah! (*business*) I thought so! Butterfly! (YAPP *falls down unconscious. Enter* BUTTERFLY)

BUTTERFLY: Here!

PUCK: Bring me Azuriel, and a wheel-barrow. Quickly.

BUTTERFLY: Quickly. (*Exit. Enter* AZURIEL)

AZURIEL: What would you with me? Is that Albion?

PUCK: No. This is a piece of humanity unguarded by intelligence, because unconscious. Listen. Cast aside your present shape, and let your spirit occupy the shape of this Policeman, which it can do, while he is unconscious.

AZURIEL: Why should I do that? (BUTTERFLY *enters with barrow*)

PUCK: Why, as a disguise—so that you may contemplate Kenna unobserved, and watch her meeting with Albion unknown to her. There never was such a chance for a jealous lover! Your thoughts and actions will be your own, but your outward shape will be a Policeman!

AZURIEL: So be it. I'll cast aside my present shape—

PUCK: Cast it into this wheel-barrow, so that I may conveniently get rid of it for you. So. Now, send your spirit into the Policeman.

EDWARD GERMAN AND BASIL HOOD

YAPP (*speaking with the manner of* AZURIEL): It is here!

PUCK (*blowing Policeman's whistle*): Are you there? Is that you, Azuriel?

YAPP: It is Azuriel who speaks to you.

PUCK: Splendid! I'll throw your old shape on the dust-heap. (*Exit with barrow*)

YAPP: The outward shape is but the rugged shell,
    The spirit is the pearl that lies therein. (PUCK *enters*)
    Swear to tell no one that Azuriel
    Goes hidden in this shape; for I perforce
    Must wear it now till sunset. Promise, Puck!
    You'll tell no one, and Kenna least of all! (*Exit*)

PUCK: I promise. I'd promise a Policeman anything. (*To* KENNA, *who enters*) There goes your Azuriel!

KENNA: In that shape?

PUCK: Yes. He is using it to spy on you. I tried to persuade him not to. Pretend you know him not, and you may make of him even more a fool than he looks.

KENNA: I have not the will to deceive him. I have not the will.

PUCK: Then follow your own will, which is a woman's wont. (*Exit. Enter* YAPP, *still as* AZURIEL)

KENNA: Welcome, Azuriel.

YAPP: You know me?

KENNA: Puck told me.

YAPP: O knavish Puck! Two-faced, two-tongued—

KENNA: Hush! Hold your one tongue, and look with your two eyes. Here comes—Albion!

YAPP: Ah! he is changed!

KENNA: Yes. Hardly would you know him—

YAPP: How do *you* know him?

KENNA: See, he wears his name upon his hat, in golden letters.

YAPP: The peacock popinjay! Now listen, Kenna! If you have any love or pity left for Albion—

KENNA: Watch. He follows a mortal maid, as you may see. See how he will make love to her, and your jealousy shall die of starvation.

YAPP: I'll watch.

Enter JOY; *she goes to seat,* JELF *following her.*

JELF: Excuse me, miss—

JOY: Yes; what is it?

JELF: Is this here your photograft, miss? (*shows photograph*)

JOY: Yes, it is. Where did you get it?

JELF: Your pa gave it to me, miss.

JOY: My father? Did he give it to you to bring to me?

JELF: He gave it to me more like to bring us together, I think, miss.

JOY: What do you mean?

JELF: Why, it was this way. Your pa, he says to me, "Jelf," he says—that's me, miss—"Jelf," he says, "have you an eye for female beauty?" he says. "Lor' love yer, sir," says I, closin' one of 'em. "Then look at this here photograft," he says; so I looks, and I says nothin', for want of fine language, as the dumb man said to the deaf when he trod on his toe. And your pa, he says, "Will you be my son-in-law?" he says. "If that's your daughter," says I. "It is," he says. Then "Done!" says I—and here I be!

JOY: I suppose you are either mad or intoxicated.

JELF: Blest if I don't think I'm a bit of both—with love and good luck.

JOY (*to* YAPP): Policeman! This man is insulting me!

JELF: Insultin' you, miss? Your pa, he says to me—

JOY: Will you please send him away?

YAPP: You love this girl?

JELF: Yes, sir. And her pa, he says—

JOY: How dare you! Do your duty, policeman, if you please.

YAPP (*to* JELF): You love this girl, and have forgotten Kenna?

JELF: Who's Kenna?

YAPP: Marry this maid by set of sun to-night—

JOY (*to* YAPP): I shall report you to the inspector for this.

YAPP: Marry this mortal maid by set of sun,
     And with the sun shall sink my jealousy
     Into the ocean of eternal time!
     And soft contentment, rising like the moon—

JOY: I shall tell the inspector that I found you incapable of doing your duty at seven o'clock in the morning (*Exit*)

YAPP: Talk not of clocks that tick your mortal hours
     And chime the knell of man's fidelity!
     A thousand years—and Kenna is forgotten!
     The swinging universe I count a clock
     To tell the moments of immortal love!
     The stars are jewels; and the flaming sun
     A ruby balance to the minute hand,
     Whose length is sun to earth. While it revolves

Immortals count a minute—men a year!
And sixty years Immortals call an hour,
A thousand years not quite a day and night!
Yet little specks of dust which men call men,
Infinitesimal (such atoms they,
So tiny, that they even hinder not
The mechanism of the Infinite),
Presume to prate of Love! O little men!
The highest wisdom mortal can attain
Is knowledge of his ignorance! Be wise! (*Exit*)

JELF: What?

Enter BLAKE.

BLAKE: How are you a-getting on, William?

JELF: Getting on? It's high time we was a-getting off. We've got into the Zoological Gardens, that's where we've got to, and the animals is loose.

BLAKE: What sort of animals do yer think you've been seein', William? Or'nary ones, or fancy?

JELF: What would you think of a policeman as was a cross between a hippopotamus and a grammerphone?

BLAKE: I should think as you'd been havin' things to drink as disagreed with you, William.

JELF: Then you'd be wrong, as usual. I ain't like you, Blake. The "happy mean's" my motter, in grog, gals, or grammerphones; as I'd have told that there young lady I'm engaged to if that there policeman hadn't interrupted us. That's what I was a-goin' to tell her—I ain't like Bill Blake, I was a-goin' to say—I ain't like Blake; the "happy mean's" my motter.

BLAKE: And a very good motter too, though I says it as shouldn't. (*Exit*)

SONG.—JELF.

A sailor man's the sort of man
As knows it is the wisest plan
To live his life as how he can
And strike a happy mean;
When he's a-settin' down to dine
He doesn't want Champagny wine—

Nor yet a pail
Of Adam's ale,
But something in between!

For it's growl a bit and grouse a bit!
A ship ain't like a house a bit!
A hammock ain't a four-post bed,
And don't behave as such!
And it swings enough when it's rough enough,
And it's ready enough to be cold enough,
And it's big enough for to hold enough
If you don't expect too much!

And when you see him on his ship
A smile a-curlin' on his lip—
He ain't a-thinkin' of the trip
But of some patch of green:
Some patch of green upon dry earth,
Enough of it to make a berth
To live his life
Him and his wife
Without the sea between!

For it's grin a bit and bear a bit
And lark a bit and swear a bit,
A sailor ain't no Sunday school
Afloat nor yet ashore!
For he sins enough, and he's rough enough,
But he's ready enough for to fight enough,
So he's wrong enough and he's right enough,
And you can't expect no more!

And when I'm stranded for a hulk,
Done all my work—or else the bulk—
I don't intend to sit and sulk,
And say "what might ha' been!"
But when my dooty's finished, why,
I'll just salute and say "Aye, aye!"
And then I'll go

Aloft—below—
Or somewheres else between.

For it's work a bit, and sleep a bit,
And sow a bit, and reap a bit,
And take the world for what it is,
And not for what it ain't!
For it's smooth enough if you're tough enough,
And it's ready enough to be found enough,
And there's sea enough and there's ground enough,
And I've got no complaint!

Enter REDDISH, BEN, *and several Fishermen.*

REDDISH: William!

JELF: Mr. Reddish, and Uncle Ben! Why, where have you
come from?

REDDISH: We were waiting at the station to meet you, William, and
saw you drive off. Me and your uncle and my Nell.

JELF: Who's Nell?

BEN: Don't you remember Mr. Reddish's niece, William? She come
the day before you went to sea, to 'ousekeep for Mr. Reddish, and
has been with him ever since.

REDDISH: Year in, year out.

JELF: Ah! I remember seeing her.

REDDISH: A good woman, William.

BEN: Remarkable.

JELF: She looked good.

BEN: Good lookin' ain't the word.

JELF: It ain't the word I used.

REDDISH: The only reason I carry this 'ere loaded pistol is to shoot the
first man as insults my Nell. To shoot him dead.

BEN: And who'd blame yer? The man as marries her will win a prize.

JELF: Then why hasn't some one gone and done it?

BEN: 'Ear the truth from her own lips. Here she comes.

Enter NELL.

REDDISH: William, this is my Nell. Nell—William.

NELL: I have heard terrible tales of your wickedness, William.

JELF: Who from?

NELL: From these men.

JELF: They're nice ones to talk.

REDDISH: They talk nice enough now, William. Different to when you was among them. And it's all doo to female influence. Tell him about it, Nell.

NELL: Are you fond of poetry, William?

JELF: No, ma'am.

NELL: Then listen—

As sunshine melts the snow
And makes the flowers grow
Doth womankind her grace bestow
Upon disgraceful Man!

(*Exit* NELL)

REDDISH: There! You've heard what she said, William.

JELF: Yes, I've heard it! What's it got to do with *me*?

REDDISH: Everything. You're the man as is goin' to marry my Nell.

JELF: Me? Marry *her*? Why?

BEN: It's like this, William. She's made up her mind to marry a bad man.

JELF: But I ain't so bad as all that!

REDDISH: You're the worst we could think of, William. You haven't the advantage of her influence as these have. Since they heard her highdears about reformin' bad men by marrying them they've turned as good as gold. But you haven't, 'cos you haven't had the chance. You've been away. You've been at sea. You haven't been under her influence.

BEN: *You* ain't teetotal, William—not yet; but you will be, when you've married to her. Imagine that.

JELF: Imagine it yourself, if you can.

REDDISH: If you thought of jilting my Nell—I don't say as you'd do it—but if the wicked thought of it came into your mind, and I saw it gleaming in your eye, I should shoot you—shoot yet dead.

BEN: And who'd blame yer?

JELF: I should! (*Exit, followed by* REDDISH *and others*)

Enter JOY *and* BROOK *opposite.*

BROOK: Joy, at last I have found you! Where have you been?

JOY: I came here as promised. But I had to go away, as I was insulted by an intoxicated sailor.

BROOK: Where is he?

JOY: I think I seem him over there with that knot of men.

BROOK: Wait here, dear. (*He is rushing off when met by* PUCK, *still wearing the appearance of* SIR JAMES JELLICOE)

PUCK: Where are you going?

BROOK: To knock down a sailor. I shall be back in a moment.

PUCK: Excuse me. Is *that* the sailor you are going to knock?

BROOK: Yes.

PUCK: I cannot allow you to do that. He is my future son-in-law.

BROOK *and* JOY: What?

PUCK: His name is William Jelf. (*To* JOY) I have chosen him as your husband, my love.

BROOK: Sir James!

PUCK: Do not interfere, sir. This is a family matter.

BROOK: You forget—

PUCK: You forget yourself.

JOY: Father, what *do* you mean? You wish me to leave the man I love and marry a common sailor?

PUCK: My child! He is a very *un*common sailor. He does not know it yet, but *I* happen to know that he is a prince. His real name is Albion—Prince Albion. If you marry him, you will be a Princess.

JOY: And if I don't?

PUCK: Observe this photograph. You will see that you have been cut off with a pair of scissors. If you oppose me, you will be cut off with a shilling, and have to live on it for the rest of your life.

BROOK: And what of that?

TRIO.—JOY, BROOK, *and* PUCK.

BROOK: If love in a cottage be all that they tell,
 In a cot will contentment reign!

PUCK: With a couple of maids to answer the bell,
 And a cook who is good, though plain.

JOY: So I'll turn up my nose at your William Jelf,
 And marry my own Brook Green!

PUCK: But you'll have to cook your dinners yourself—
 Do you know what that will mean?

 It will mean that you find that you somehow fail
 With the soup, which you meant to be "thick ox-tail,"
 For it comes out thin and extremely pale;
 And you give the potatoes a hopeless prod,
 But they *won't* get soft; and the fish, a cod,

May taste very nice, but it *looks* so odd,
As (being a slippery sort of fish)
It fell on the fender off the dish—
Not quite what a first-rate cook would wish!
And it's boiled too little, or else too long
(You are not sure which, but there's something wrong);
And the joint has acquired the usual sin
Of a burnt outside and a raw within,
And as for the pudding, you're free from doubt
How that "will turn out"—for it *won't* "turn out"—
For your fingers fumble the steaming string,
And when you undo it, the cloth will cling,
And the pudding appears like a shapeless mass
That's been out in the rain all night on the grass!
And you say, "What a meal this meal might be
If it hadn't been cooked by a cook like me."
And that is the sort of dinner I mean
Will be swallowed by you and your own Brook Green—
By Mister and Missus Green!

BROOK: Then for dinners our course will be "stick to a stock
    Of kisses and bread and cheese!"

PUCK: But for breakfast and dinner you must wear a frock,
    Tho' as simple and cheap as you please!

JOY: If I turn up my nose at your William Jelf
    And marry my own Brook Green—

PUCK: You will have to make your dresses yourself,
    Do you know what that will mean?

It will mean that you suddenly hear the gong,
And the dress you have made has all gone wrong!
For the skirt's too short, and the sleeves too long!
And the bodice too big, and overlaps,
Or else it is far too small, perhaps;
And you tug it together, and something snaps!
And there isn't a hook that will meet an eye,
And if ever they did, they'd be sure to fly,
If you happened to sneeze, or laugh, or sigh;
And you can't put your hand on a single pin,
But you suddenly do, and the point goes in,

And you have you wait till the bleeding stops,
And just as it does so something *pops*,
And you look in the glass, and are shocked to see
The "neck" you designed as a harmless "V,"
For though designed a "V," the dread-
Ful thing looks more like an X.Y.Z.,
Or anything else in the alphabet;
So you fill in the "V" with a "chemisette"
Which you hastily try to improvise
From a couple of handkerchiefs (*lady's size*),
And that is the dowdy dress I mean
You will wear if you care to be Mrs. Green—
To be Mister and Missus Green!
(*this verse does not appear in the vocal score*)

BROOK: If servants we cannot afford to employ,
    We can wait on ourselves, you see—
PUCK: And scrubbing the floors you may rather enjoy
    Till you suffer from "housemaid's knee"!
JOY: If I turn up my nose at your William Jelf,
    And marry my own Brook Green—
PUCK: You will have to do the housework yourself—
    Do you know what that will mean?

It will mean that you both of you bravely fix
To rise in the morning at half-past six,
So you set the alarum—and then it sticks,
And it doesn't go off, and you sleep till eight!
You've to catch a train and are bound to be late
Unless you can dress at a fearful rate!
You jump out of bed, and hastily throw
A dressing-gown on and your hair done *so*,
You fly downstairs to the kitchen below,
And you light the fire and of course it smokes,
And you sneeze and you cough, and between your chokes,
You suddenly give a piercing yell
Because you have noticed a black beet-*el!*
And the smoke and the scream of course conspire
To make you believe the house is on fire!
So you rush downstairs, half out of your mind,

With a jugful of water, and then you find
That you've thrown it on *her*, and she
Is as much put out as a fire could be!
And the matter results, as a matter of course,
In a separation, or else divorce!
And that is the kind of life I mean
Will be led by the wife of your own Brook Green—
By Mister and Missus Green!

Exit PUCK.

BROOK: I think your father has suddenly gone mad. He is suffering from sunstroke. Perhaps he forgot to wet his head when he was bathing.

JOY: Yet there is some sense in what he said.

BROOK: Sense!

JOY: If I marry against his wish, he will certainly cut me off with a shilling, and—you are not rich, dear, are you?

BROOK: I have a pound in the Post Office, besides the one I get every week.

JOY: With my shilling it will be a guinea, for the first week. I am afraid a guinea won't take one very far.

BROOK: It will take *two* as far as Fairyland, if they are the right two.

JOY: I am thinking of you. Bread and cheese and kisses are enough for me. But suppose we have no bread?

BROOK: We could have toast—I prefer it; so *that* would be all right.

JOY: It would be all wrong. I am thinking of you—

BROOK: Are you sure?

JOY: Believe what you like.

BROOK: I am sorry to say I believe what I dislike. I heard your father tell you that sailor is really a prince. I have always looked up to you as a princess.

JOY: And now you look down upon me for wanting to be one?

BROOK: Oh, I don't say that. But I have learned something of women in the last five minutes.

JOY: Have you? Then you deserve to be taught another lesson.

BROOK: What do you mean?

JOY: You shall see. I won't be doubted for nothing!

Enter KENNA, TITANIA *and others.* KENNA *brings on* JELF.

EDWARD GERMAN AND BASIL HOOD

Act 1 Finale.—Ensemble

JOY: Till the day
    Of my majority
    I'll obey
    Papa's authority!
    Oh, how can I face my father's wrath
    In the days of my minority!
KENNA: To obey
    Those in authority
    Is the way
    Of the majority;
    And how can you brave paternal wrath
    In the days of meek minority!
JELF: To obey
    Papa's authority
    Is the way
    Of the majority:
    But she will incur her father's wrath
    If she joins the mad majority!

Ensemble.

{   BROOK: Oh, a pin
{   For his authority!
{   Tho' I'm in
{   A small minority,
{   Too many cooks will spoil the broth,
{   So a fig for a big majority!
{   JOY: Till the day of my majority, etc.
{   JELF: To obey Papa's authority, etc.
{   KENNA *and* CHORUS: To obey those in authority, etc.
JELF: Cost what it may
    I'll help her to obey!
    I'll sweat I love her, though it be a banger!
    It must be right
    Because it is polite
    To save a lady from her father's anger!
CHORUS: It must be right, etc.

KENNA (*to* JOY): Accept your fortune, come what will,
　　Although it prove a bitter pill!
　　Think of your father, think not of yourself,
　　And marry William Jelf!
CHORUS: And marry William Jelf!

ENSEMBLE.

{　JELF: Accept my fortune, that I will,
{　　　For every Jack must have a Jill!
{　　　And I'll not leave a lady on the shelf—
{　　　That isn't William Jelf!
{　JOY: Accept my fortune, if you will,
{　　　The takings of my father's till!
{　　　Take all the takings, then take yourself away!
{　KENNA: Accept your fortune, come what will, etc.
{　OTHERS: Accept his fortune, that he will!
{　　　For every Jack must have a Jill!
{　　　And he'll not leave a lady on the shelf—
{　　　That isn't William Jelf!
JELF: I'll marry you! I'll marry you!
{　KENNA *and* CHORUS: He'll marry her!
{　JOY: He'll marry me!
{　BROOK: Ungrateful cur!
JELF: Whate'er my fate, I'll face it;
　　This is my opportunitee,
　　And thus do I embrace it! (*Embraces* JOY)
CHORUS: He'll marry her! He'll marry her!
　　Whate'er his fate, he'll face it;
　　This is his opportunitee,
　　And now will he embrace it!
JELF: I'll marry you! (*Dance*)
CHORUS: Whate'er his fate, he'll face it!
BROOK: Unclasp her, ruffian, or die!
JOY: Nay, 'tis my father's wish! Good-bye!
　　Good-bye! Good-bye!
BROOK: Good-bye,
　　Good-bye—
　　A little word,

And lightly said!
When it is heard!
And Angel Hope her wings doth spread,
Each wing a fluttering sigh,
To bear the soul of what lies dead
To some pure star on high!
CHORUS: And Angel Hope, etc.
BROOK: I go!
But no one knows
Whither or where I fly!
But no one knows
Whether to live or die!
CHORUS: He goes!
But no one knows
Whether to live or die!
And Angel Hope, etc.
Exit BROOK.
JOY *pretends to faint and is held in* JELF's *arms.*
Enter REDDISH. *Picture.*
REDDISH: What's this! Can I my senses doubt!
Why, bless me! what's the man about!
KENNA: His arm's about a slender waist—
His lips about her lips to taste—
And *he's* about this maid to wed.
REDDISH: Contrariwise! Alive or dead
He'll wed my Nell—for so he said!
MEN: To marry Nell he promised!
REDDISH: He'll wed my Nell alive or dead!
MEN: To marry Nell he promised!
REDDISH: And if anybody hurts her pride,
He'll find he's suddenly died
Of his bullets in his inside;
He can start a-ringin' his funeral bell
If he means for to jilt my Nell!
CHORUS: And if anybody hurts her pride, etc.
JELF: 'Tis true! too true!
I've promised two!
Can I to two be true!
What shall I do?

When I was told
This maid was mine
Whose heart is gold
In human shrine,
I felt that struck
With my good luck
I stammered like a dumb thing!
My tongue refused
It's usual work,
Although not used
A job to shirk;
And though they knew
What they should do
My lips neglected something!

CHORUS: His lips neglected something!

JELF: And this is what
They should have said—
That I have got
To go and wed
Another gell
Whose name is Nell,
So I'm engaged to either!
And I'm aware
They both love me,
But I'll be fair
As fair can be;
And as I'm loth
To marry both—
I'll up and marry neither!

CHORUS: He will not marry either!

JELF: For evermore
A bachelor,
I'll be as I have been before.
For evermore a bacehelor,
I will not marry, marry either!

KENNA: He will not marry either! He will not marry either!
Our plot has failed!

{ Chorus: Our plot has miscarried,
{   If he isn't married,
{   By seven o'clock tonight,
{   And what shall we tell
{   Azuriel?
{   He'll punish you with a lifelong spell—
{   Oh, pity a Fairy's plight!
{ Kenna: Our plot has miscarried,
{   If he isn't married,
{   By seven o'clock tonight,
{   And what shall we tell
{   Azuriel?
{   He'll punish then with a lifelong spell—
{   Oh, pity a Fairy's plight!
{ Joy: If Brook had but tarried,
{   We might have been married,
{   Oh! where has he ta'en his flight.
{   If he hadn't been jea-
{   lous, and mad as well
{   We might have been ringing our marriage bell,
{   Oh, pity a maiden's plight!
{ Jelf: A man till he's married
{   Is hampered and harried
{   On doing the thing that's right!
{   And I can't marry Nell,
{   And *her* as well,
{   For they'd punish you then with a five-year spell,
{   For trying to be polite!

Kenna (*spoken*): Puck! Come to my aid! Where are you, Puck?
Enter Puck, *disguised*.

Recitative.—Puck.

Allow me, if convenient, to introduce myself:
I am Sir Robin Goodfellow: Sir Robin—Mr. Jelf!
I am a Judge of Admiralty, Probate, and Divorce,
And I fancy I can show how to steer a proper course.

Your delicate dilemma must appeal with tragic force
To any Judge of Admiralty—let alone Divorce!

SONG.—PUCK.

A bachelor of navel cut
Determines that with *no* bait
Will he be hooked in marriage, but
He meets a Judge of Probate!
That Judge remarks, "If that's your will,
I very much regret it,
For Cupid is a codicil
While will, I think, upset it!

For Cupid's comprehensive clause
Will catch you, bait or no bait
(I know that I am right, because
I am a Judge of Probate!)
CHORUS: For Cupid's comprehensive clause, etc.
PUCK: From Probate now I lightly trip
(Though you'll not catch me tripping)
To show my close acquaintanceship
With Marriages, and Shipping!
A person of the sailor sort
(And you, I fancy, are one)
Should have a wife in every port,
Unless a singu*lar* one!

It is, I think, a usual course,
And not considered faulty
(If judged according to Divorce,
As well as Admiralty!)
CHORUS: It is, I think, a usual course, etc.
PUCK: But if you marry twice, the chance
Is *one* wife is the prior:
And that's the only circumstance
In bigamy to sigh o'er!
So it is clear to any dunce
(Or will be when I've said it)

You've got to marry both at once,
To marry, sir, with credit!

That is, I think, the only plan,
And you will never rue it:
If you can find a clergyman
Whose willing for to do it!
CHORUS: So now, as quickly as we can,
The time to make a start is—
To try and find a clergyman
Who'll marry all the parties.
Picture.

CURTAIN

Act II

Afternoon of the same day.

The Scene represents a small fishing village. The houses run up both sides of stage in a street, and at back is seen a view of the sea. On the left is the Inn. It is late afternoon. Brilliant sunshine.

BEN *and* DOUBLEDAY *are discovered sitting under tree in front of the Inn.* BEN *is asleep. Chorus of Men heard off, as if on beach.*

CHORUS: High and dry
    Let her lie,
    Haul O!
    On her side
    Let her bide,
    Haul O!
    And the tide may ebb, and the tide may flow,
    And the wind may blow-ow-ow-ow!
    Yeo ho! Heave ho! Yeo ho!
The Fairies enter. They are dressed as fishermen and fishergirls.
MEN: We're no longer bakers,
    Or candlestick makers,
    Or members of any such trade.
GIRLS: You're no longer able
    Our calling to label
    As that of a nursery-maid!
ALL: Yet nobody guesses
    (Because of our dresses)
    That we are a Faerie Choir!
    Oh, no one aware is
    We're nothing but fairies
    Parading in fishers' attire!
ZEPHYRUS (*addressing* BEN *and* DOUBLEDAY): Hail, mortals! We are Fairies!
A FAIRY: Oh, hush!
ZEPHYRUS: They'll not believe it! (DOUBLEDAY *nudges* BEN *and wakes him*)
DOUBLEDAY: Did you hear w-w-what he s-s-said, Ben?

EDWARD GERMAN AND BASIL HOOD

BEN: Eh? I was asleep—dreamin'. Such a beautiful dream, too. All about barrels of beer. There was barrels and barrels and barrels. What did you wake me up for?

ZEPHYRUS: What place is this?

BEN: This? Why this is the Alehouse; leastways it *was* a alehouse till Mr. Reddish's niece come and turned it teetotal temp'rance topsy-turvy. The Alehouse—that's what this is, or ought to be—the Alehouse.

ZEPHYRUS: What is an alehouse?

BEN: What's *what*?

ZEPHYRUS: What is an alehouse?

BEN: Wait a minute. (*Calling excitedly*) Mr. Reddish! Mr. Reddish!

Enter REDDISH.

REDDISH: What is it?

BEN: Why, it's a chap askin' what a—hear him for yourself. (*To* ZEPHYRUS) Let Mr. Reddish hear yer say it.

REDDISH: What do you want?

ZEPHYRUS: I want to know what an alehouse is!

REDDISH: Oh, do you? Now, look here, my lad, none of your chaff with me. It's bad enough to have a niece turn your "Jolly Tar" into "Jolly Teapot" without having it thrown in your face. It don't bear joking about. Do you tumble?

ZEPHYRUS: Tumble? We seldom tumble! Kenna is the only one of us who has tumbled from her proper station; she was a cloud, and was betrothed to a mountain; she was foolish, and fell to earth in tears of rain. And so Prince Albion saw her, and loved her. But she will satisfy Azuriel that his jealousy is unfounded, and then she will become a cloud again.

REDDISH: What the deuce are you talking about? And where do you come from?

ZEPHYRUS: We suit ourselves to our surroundings. Now we are fisher-folk. But it is only one Midsummer Day that we appear like this.

REDDISH: A good day to choose for oilskins; I suppose this is what's meant by Midsummer mad. That's what they are—mad, poor things! mad! silly!

DOUBLEDAY: He said they w-w-were F-f-f-f—

REDDISH: Fisher-folk. I heard him. But what on earth are they don' in their oilskings weather like this, without a cloud in the sky?

ZEPHYRUS: Kenna will be a cloud in the sky again soon. Here she comes.

REDDISH: Come along. It ain't safe here. (*Exeunt*)

Enter KENNA.

SONG.—KENNA.

A Mountain stood like a grim outpost—
The sentinel of a mighty host;
In sun and storm, by night or day,
A tireless veteran grim and grey!
A soft white Cloud was the Mountain's bride—
She nestled close to her husband's side:
For though the Mountain was grey and grim,
That pretty white Cloud felt drawn to him!

But the Mountain stared to his front,
Like a soldier, bold and blunt!
And by mountain laws it is not allow'd
For a peak to speak to a passing cloud,
Never! Never! Never!

He stood stock still and he spake no word
Which the Cloud, his bride, considered absurd,
Oh! grim and grey like a rock he stood,
As a soldier bold (*or boulder*) should!
So she thought it due to her self-respect
To show contempt for his rude neglect,
And she sailed away with an air of "pooh"
The very first breeze between the two!

And the Mountain bore the affront
Like a soldier bold and blunt,
But he said to himself (*tho' not aloud*),
"I'll never forgive that faithless Cloud,
Never, never, never!"

KENNA: Welcome, Fairies. Is Azuriel with you?

ZEPHYRUS: A little way behind. The habit of a policeman is a drawback to quick travel.

FAIRY: Here he is.

Enter AZURIEL, *in the shape of* YAPP. *Exit Chorus, gradually.*

YAPP: Kenna, it is an hour to sunset. Is Albion married?

KENNA: Not yet.

YAPP: Why not?

KENNA: There is a difficulty concerning his marriage with two ladies at the same time.

YAPP: The more you make him marry, the more will I believe in you.

KENNA: Yes. But he can't find a clergyman to do it. And he must be married by a clergyman.

(*Enter* PUCK)

PUCK: Or a Registrar. I am the Registrar.

YAPP: Look!

KENNA: What do you see?

YAPP: Two Albions! Two men with Albion written on their hats.

PUCK: Quite so. That is the real one's method of preserving his incognito. No one can tell which is which—which is the right one and which is not.

YAPP: Which is the right?

PUCK: The left.

YAPP: How do *you* know?

PUCK: A little bird told me.

YAPP: Will the bird tell *me*?

PUCK: If you go and ask it?

YAPP: Where is it?

PUCK: I will tell you.

SONG.—PUCK.

By a Piccadilly cab-stand
At the corner of a street,
I heard a London sparrow
Singing "Tweet, tweet, tweet!"
And I listened willy-nilly,
While the little sparrow sang
His song of Piccadilly
With a little cockney twang!

And the bird sang "Tweet!
Have you heard the news?
I can tell you *such* a secret,
Half a dozen if I choose!
For I pick up information
From the cabmen in the street,
And among their chaff sometimes you'll find
A grain of two of wheat, to ear—tweet!"

So I said, "Oh, Mr. Sparrow,
Have you anything to say
On certain burning questions
Which are topics of the day?
Can you tell me if our Navy
Has its complement of guns?
Or must we cry 'Peccavi'
To the tune of many tons?"

And the bird said, "Tweet!
You haven't heard the news:
We have the ships, and money too,
But haven't any crews.
And I heard a cabman saying
That to underman the Fleet
Was like a dinner party when
There's nothing there to eat—tweet, tweet!"

(*the rest of the lyrics do not appear in the vocal score*)
Then I said, "Dear Mr. Sparrow,
Can you tell me why the hue
Of a Parliamentary Blue-book
Should be *blue*—and is it true
It's a delicate suggestion
Of the language of debate,
When there's any little question
Re a disunited state?"

And the bird said, "Tweet!
I fear I must refuse

To repeat the sort of language
That the Irish Party use!
But I heard a cabman saying
'When that Irish party meet,
They stand upon their dignity—
With very muddy feet'—tweet, tweet!"

Then I said "Observant Sparrow,
Will you give me, if you can,
Your deliberate opinion
Of the British working man?
And if foreign competition
Is a thing that he dislikes
Does it strike you his position
Is improved at all by strikes?"

And the bird said, "Tweet!
I think, upon my soul,
That our working men prefer a loaf
To any other *role*!
And I heard a cabman saying,
'When they hang about the street
And talk of competition, why
The deuce they don't compete!'—tweet, tweet!"

PUCK: Now go back to London and find that bird. Fly!

YAPP: I cannot fly in this slow-moving shape.

PUCK: True. It would be asking too much. Return to your own shape,
and let your spirit leave this policeman's body, and his own intellect
return to it, such as it is.

YAPP: So be it. Farewell.

PUCK: Good-bye! (*The Policeman's expression changes, he appears dazed,
and the manner of* YAPP *returns to him*)

YAPP: Why, what am I doin' here?

PUCK: I think you were running after a thief who had stolen a
gentleman's clothes when he was bathing.

YAPP: Why, so I was.

PUCK: Then you fainted.

YAPP: Why, so I did.

PUCK: He went *that* way. Hurry!

YAPP: Why, so I am. (*Exit* YAPP, *hurrying slowly.* PUCK *goes to Inn and rings the bell*)

Enter RECRUITING SERGEANT *and* BEN.

BEN: Yes, this is Winklemouth, Recruitin' Sergeant; this is Winklemouth. And that's the Alehouse.

SERGEANT: And where shall I find any likely young men?

BEN: There ain't none.

SERGEANT: Why?

BEN: Why, they've all left the neighbourhood since Mr. Reddish's niece come and turned the Alehouse teetotal topsy-turvy. There ain't no likely men left—'tain't likely. (*He sits under tree*) Barrels and barrels there was.

SERGEANT: Barrels of what?

BEN: Why, what would they be? Hunderds, did I say? Why, there was thousands! And he woke me up! Drat him! (*Composes himself to sleep. Exit* SERGEANT)

JOY *opens door of Inn and enters.*

JOY: Did you ring?

PUCK: Are you the servant?

JOY: Why?

PUCK: I believe I recognize you as the daughter of an acquaintance of mine. Sir James Jellicoe of Jellicoe & Co.

JOY: It is quite true. My father ordered me to marry a man I do not love, and rather than do that I have accepted a place as servant, and my mistress is going to marry the man my father wishes me to marry. I have made that arrangement with her, and have telegraphed my father to tell him.

PUCK: Dear, dear! Is your mistress at home?

JOY: What do you want?

PUCK: Will you tell her that the Registrar has called?

JOY: Yes. What shall I tell her you've called for?

PUCK: So as to let her know,

JOY: To let her know what?

PUCK: That the Registrar has called.

JOY: Yes; but *why*?

PUCK: Why, to let her know!

JOY: But what shall I say you called *about*?

PUCK: Say I've called about half-past six.

JOY: But *what* shall I tell her you've called for.

PUCK: Because if you *don't* tell her she won't know.

JOY: What I mean is, shall I mention your business?

PUCK: Certainly. Tell her the Registrar has called.

JOY: But having told her you have called, what shall I tell her you have called *about*?

PUCK: About twenty minutes to seven now.

JOY: But what is it you want?

PUCK: A glass of stout.

JOY: We don't keep it.

PUCK: Thank you. (JOY *exit and shuts door.* PUCK *breaks a flower-pot, then rings bell and exit.* BEN *wakes. Enter* SERGEANT)

SERGEANT: Why do they keep the door to that inn shut? To keep people outside?

BEN: To keep 'em inside, I expecks. Nothing else would. They sells nothin' but lemonade. Let me go to sleep and forget it all. Barrels and barrels and barrels—and me shut in with 'em! Me! (*He sleeps*)

Enter JOY.

JOY (*to Sergeant*): Did you ring?

SERGEANT: No, my dear.

JOY: Don't call me "my dear," please.

SERGEANT: Don't go.

JOY: What do you want?

SERGEANT: I want to know where the likely young men are.

JOY: How should I know?

SERGEANT: Well, if you don't, who should—that's what I'd like to know.

JOY: You will kindly understand that I am not an ordinary servant girl. When my mistress marries I am going to remain here as housekeeper; and then at the end of a year or so, when I have thoroughly learned the duties of a household, I shall be able to make the man I love a comfortable home, even though we cannot afford a servant. That is why I am here. Now perhaps you will treat me properly.

SERGEANT: Here goes. If I ask you to let *me* be the man you love, what will you say?

JOY: *That*! (*She smacks his face*)

SERGEANT: I say, that's my cheek!

JOY: That's what *I* say. (*Exit and shuts door*)

SERGEANT: In ladylike language.

(*Enter* Reddish)

SERGEANT (*to Reddish*): Now, my lad, why don't you join the Marines?

REDDISH: What for?

SERGEANT: To make you grow.

REDDISH: If I look more like a shrunken shadder than a man, it's because—hush!

(*Enter* NELL)

NELL: What are you talking about, Uncle Reddish?

REDDISH: About this here flower-pot, Nell. It seems to be broke.

NELL: Who broke it? (*To* SERGEANT) Was it you?

SERGEANT: What should I want to go about breaking flower-pots for?

NELL: I can believe any man capable of anything, even the deliberate destruction of innocent flower-pots. Are you married?

SERGEANT: Why?

NELL: Marriage makes a vast difference to men.

SERGEANT: Yes, ma'am. I've tried it.

NELL: That's a pity.

SERGEANT: So *I* say. (*Exit*)

REDDISH: What I want to know is—(*Enter* PUCK) How did this here favourite flower-pot of mine come to get broke?

PUCK: *My* theory is that it fell down, so. (*Drops another*)

REDDISH: What do you mean by that?

PUCK: I mean that I should think that it tumbled down, thus. (*Knocks over another*) Of course I am open to contradiction. But that is what I should say—that someone deliberately threw it down, like this. (*Breaks another*)

REDDISH: What are you doin'? Let go of that flower-pot.

PUCK: With pleasure. (*Drops it*) I am the Registrar. (*To* NELL) I am here to marry you, by sunset.

REDDISH (*to Puck*): If you do that you can break as many as you like. (*Enters house*)

PUCK: I propose—

NELL: I cannot listen. I am engaged to William.

PUCK: Pardon me. My proposal is to marry you to William in my capacity of Registar.

(*Enter* JELF *and* BLAKE)

NELL: I have just arranged that the clergyman shall marry me—

JELF: Hooray for the clergyman!

NELL: I mean that the clergyman shall marry me to you.

JELF: Why don't women say what they mean at once.

PUCK (*with flower-pot*): I was advised by Sir Robin Goodfellow, whom I think you met this morning—

JELF: It was him who made all the mischief.

PUCK: Mischief, my dear sir! You surprise me! (*Drops flower-pot. REDDISH hands him another one, and beckons JOY to remove broken bits*)

JELF: Yes. It was him who laid down the law as it was right for a sailor to marry two young women at once.

PUCK: And who dares contradict him?

JELF: Both the young women?

JOY: I for one.

NELL: And I for the other.

PUCK: Well, as long as you *do* marry, it doesn't matter to me *which* you marry.

JELF: Oh, don't it?

PUCK: No, not to me, as Registrar.

JELF: Well, it does to me—as bridegroom!

REDDISH: All that I insists on is that my Nell is the one that's married, and taken away.

PUCK: And all I insist on is that you are married in your right name.

BLAKE: I always says as every time a sailor's married in a wrong name he ain't married at all. That's kept a lot o' sailors from marryin'—leastways, from bein' married.

PUCK: Quite so. And that brings me to the point. (*To JELF*) I believe you are not aware that you are a prince?

ALL: Eh?

JELF: A what?

PUCK: A prince.

JELF: Spell it.

PUCK: A-L-B-I-O-N. That is your name, sir—or, at any rate, your surname. Why, nobody seems aware of it.

JOY: I am. (*To JELF*) My father told me. That's why he wants me to marry you. But I wouldn't if you were fifty princes rolled into one disguise—because I love someone else! So there! (*Exit*)

PUCK: There. Do you understand?

JELF: No, I'm blessed if I do.

Enter KENNA.

PUCK: You will—when you have heard the remarkable story which
this gipsy has told me, and we are going to tell you.

TRIO.—KENNA, PUCK, *and* JELF, *with* CHORUS.

KENNA: If you will spare the time,
I'll give you a recital
Of how you came
To lose your name,
Your property, and title!
PUCK: The dreadful tale of crime
Proceeding from her lips is
Entirely true,
And tells how you
Were carried off by gipsies.
JELF: By gipsies?
PUCK: By gipsies,
By interfering gipsies!
KENNA *and* PUCK: When you were a child of less than two
A terrible wrong was done to you!
For you lived in a palace extremely grand
Till carried away be a gipsy band!
(CHORUS *entering, having changed their Fairy dresses*)
CHORUS: And we're that very identical band!
Lurking, luckily, pluckily near at hand!
Ready to swear the tale is true—
The terrible tale they're telling you!
Life entrancing,
Singing, dancing!
Steal a child or two!
That's the kind
Of life you'll find
Is led by a gipsy crew! (*Exeunt* CHORUS)
KENNA: One morning, having fed
On bottled milk and water,
You soundly slept
And up I crept—
A gipsy's little daughter!

PUCK: The nursemaid turned her head,
    To view a soldier strapping;
    And as she did
    That gipsy kid
    Came up and caught you napping!
JELF: Kidnapping!
PUCK: Kidnapping!
    A gipsy kid, kidnapping!
KENNA *and* PUCK: And I / she was that gipsy child (*or kid*),
    By rascally instinct bad (*or bid*);
    I/She carried you off to my/her gipsy band,
    Who were luckily lurking near at hand! (*Exit* PUCK)
CHORUS (*re-entering*): And we, you'll readily understand,
    Are that identical gipsy band!
    And solemnly say the story's true,
    The terrible story she's told to you!
    Singing, dancing,
    Life entrancing,
    Steal a child or two!
    That's the kind
    Of life you'll find
    Is led by a gipsy crew!

Dance.

BLAKE: It's an eggstraordinary story.
JELF (*to* KENNA): Look here. You're not much more than
    twenty—do you mean to tell me you carried me off when
    I was a babby?
KENNA: Perhaps I should not have told you that. I—I meant
    to say that I know you *were* carried off. I have been told the
    story.
JELF: Who told you?
KENNA: A little bird told me.
JELF: What sort of bird?
BLAKE: It might have been a parrot.
JELF: Or a lyre-bird. They carry funny tails.
BLAKE: Talkin' of parrots—
JELF: We ain't. What about this lyre-bird?
KENNA: Do you mean that you disbelieve all those witnesses, and
    won't acknowledge that you are Prince Albion?

JELF: I mean that the tale that was carried by that there bird is the sort o' tale that wants a grain o' salt puttin' on it.

KENNA: Will nothing induce you to be married in the name of Albion?

JELF: Wait a bit. (*To* BLAKE) Is it true that if a chap marries in his wrong name he ain't married at all?

BLAKE: In course it is.

JELF: Have you known it tried in law?

BLAKE: I've knowed it tried in the Navy.

JELF (*to* KENNA): I'll say I'm that there Prince if I marries that there Nell.

KENNA: You will?

JELF: Yes. You can trust a sailor's word when he gives it to a lady.

(*Enter* AZURIEL, *in his own shape*)

KENNA: Here is Azuriel. You know Azuriel?

JELF: How do you do, sir?

AZURIEL: Are you Prince Albion?

JELF: That's me. Who might *you* be?

KENNA: Do you forget Azuriel, who wanted to kill you because you wanted to marry me?

JELF: When?

KENNA: A thousand years ago.

JELF: Oh yes. (*To* BLAKE) Come on, Bill. It was the Zoological Gardens this mornin', and now it's a open air lunatic asylum.
(*Exeunt* JELF *and* BLAKE)

KENNA: Do you believe me now?

AZURIEL: Yes.

(*Enter* FAIRIES, *then* OBERON *and* TITANIA)

BRIDAL CHORUS AND DUET.

See a rainbow arch
Joineth sun and shade!
'Tis the bridge where Oberon
Leads his cavalcade.
Sound a Bridal March,
Love hath come again
For Kenna and Azuriel,
And Joy hath conquered Pain!

Solo.—Azuriel.

Nature, sound thy diapason,
Let thy thousand thousand voices
Join in praise of Love Triumphant—
Love hath come again!
Chorus: Nature, sound thy diapason, etc.

Duet.—Kenna *and* Azuriel.

Ye silver chimes of fall and fountain,
Ring out from mountain unto mountain!
O west wind, spread thy rushing wings,
To bear the anthem Nature sings!
Chorus: Ye silver chimes of fall and fountain, etc.
  (*this verse does not appear in the vocal score*)
  Ye birds, o'er field and forest flying,
  Show'r golden song upon him hieing,
  To counterpoise the thunder note
  That rolls from Ocean's mighty throat!
  (*the vocal score continues with the following chorus*)
  Sound a Bridal March,
  Love hath come again
  For Kenna and Azuriel,
  And Joy hath conquered Pain!
All exeunt except Kenna, Azuriel, Oberon, *and* Titania.
Titania: All has ended happily for Kenna! (*Kisses her*)
Oberon: Come!
Kenna: Stay. In my own joy I would not forget the unhappiness of
    others. Puck!
(*Enter* Puck)
Puck: Here.
Kenna: You know how we have used these mortal lovers?
Puck: Well; or rather ill; or rather—I know well how we have used
    them ill.
Kenna: I would not break their hearts to mend my own. Set things
    right for them.
Oberon: See to it. Come.
Puck: Here, wait a bit! Won't you wait and help me?

KENNA: I'll wait.

AZURIEL: And I with you.

OBERON: How long will it take?

PUCK: To make half-a-dozen lovers happy? Half-an-hour at least.

OBERON: So be it. We'll not go yet. Come. (*Exit with* TITANIA)

(*Enter* BROOK; *he is disguised as a Boatman*)

PUCK: Pardon me, sir—you look depressed. Positively suicidal. Are you contemplating marriage?

BROOK: Mind your own business.

PUCK: I am. I am the Registrar.

BROOK: I shall never marry. Marriage is a target where man can never hit happiness—

PUCK: Because of the misses—don't say that, sir.

BROOK: I shall say nothing more to you. And I particularly wish to be left alone.

PUCK: You won't let me help you over this matter?

BROOK: I shall help you over that sea wall if you annoy me.

PUCK: Very well. If you won't, you won't. Excuse me. Do you know if those boats at the pier-head are for sale? My name is Pierhead Morgan. (*Exeunt* PUCK *and* KENNA)

SONG.—BROOK.

(*this song was replaced during the original run, with lyrics which appear the end of this libretto*)

A blue sky and a blue sea
Tho' others call them gray;
For love shone down on you and me,
And made a summer's day.
Then I was yours and you were mine,
And all the world was ours,
And our hearts were gay as fields in May,
For all our thoughts were flowers!

Then gather them while you may,
And bind them for your maid;
And let a sprig of rosemarie
Be in the garland laid!
For flowers, alas! do fade and pass,

And men and maids do part,
Then gather a sprig of rosemarie
To grace your lady's heart!

A gray sky and a gray sea,
Tho' other count them blue;
For you have gone away from me,
And summer goes with you!
And no more garlands I do twine
To crown your dainty head;
For my heart is bare as a garden fair
Where all the flowers lie dead!

Then gather them while you may,
And bind them with a vow;
And set a sprig of rosemarie
Within the garland now!
For flowers, alas! do fade and pass,
And men and maids do part,
Oh, spare me the sprig of rosemarie
I set upon your heart!

Exit. Enter PUCK. *Enter* JELF.

PUCK: Pardon me, you look cast down. Is it because you are going to marry the wrong lady, or because you are not going to marry the right one?

JELF: You seem to take a deal of interest in my marryin'.

PUCK: As Registrar. Whom do you want to marry?

JELF: The young lady I'm engaged to.

PUCK: Which one?

JELF: What I say—the young one.

PUCK: Miss Joy Jellicoe. Excuse me. I'll take a few notes. (*Fetches large slate from side of Inn, on which is written the amount of subscriptions to "Nell's Wedding Present."*) Now, what do you consider the chief obstacles to your union with Miss Jellicoe?

JELF: Well, one obstacle is her lovin' another chap who's follered her here—because I've seen him dressed as a boatman.

PUCK: She has thrown him over, and he feels upset. It will be easy to get rid of him.

JELF: Couldn't that there gipsy band carry him off?

PUCK: That's not a bad idea of yours; but a military band would have more brass. He shall be carried away by martial music. Butterfly! (BUTTERFLY *enters*)

BUTTERFLY: Here!

PUCK: Provide me with a military brass band, with drum-major's uniform complete. Quickly.

BUTTERFLY: Quickly. (*Exit.* JELF *turns to look after her, and* PUCK *disappears*)

JELF (*alarmed*): Blake!

PUCK (*returning*): Yes, William. Is there any other obstacle?

JELF: Of course there's the obstacle of my marryin' Nell.

PUCK: Someone else must marry Nell.

JELF: There's Bill Blake might do it—he saved my life once before; but then he's a sensible chap, too. Besides, she's bent now on marryin' a prince, like me.

PUCK: Bill Blake must be the prince.

JELF: In place of me?

PUCK: In place of you. We will now point out to Nell the desirability of marrying a prince, whoever he is. Here she comes. (*Enter* NELL) Pardon me—have you ever pondered on the inestimable advantages that would accrue to Society if a woman of your stamp were to marry a prince? Have you ever weighed this matter, ma'am?

NELL: Frequently.

TRIO.—NELL, PUCK, *and* JELF.

NELL: A German Prince
　　May wed me since
　　A single woman still I am!
PUCK: Then lager beer
　　Will disappear
　　From the realms of Kaiser William!
NELL: For drinking I condemn,
　　And a lager-loving German
　　I would not brook until he took
　　To water like a Merman!

　　For I consider lager wrong,
　　And Germans drink it all day long;

A state of things that would not be
If the country had to deal with me!
PUCK *and* JELF: Oh, she considers lager wrong,
  And Germans drink it all day long;
  A thing, perhaps, that wouldn't occur
  If they had to sit and drink with her.
NELL: Give me a chance
  Of saving France
  By marrying the President!
JELF: In gay Paree
  You'd have to be
  A most unwilling resident!
NELL: No more the gay can-can
  Should Frenchmen find entrancing,
  For I should make the country wake
  To wholesome dread of dancing.

  For I have heard that all day long
  All Frenchmen dance the mad cong-cong;
  A state of things that would not be,
  If their country had to deal with *me*!
PUCK *and* JELF: Oh, she has heard that all day long
  All Frenchmen dance the mad cong-cong;
  A state of things that wouldn't occur
  If they had to dance that dance with *her*!
NELL: And if, again,
  The King of Spain
  Should send his ambassadors
PUCK: To say "Tra la"
  To my papa,
  "Our King your little lass adores."
NELL: No more the gay guitar
  Through Spain should tinkle-tankle,
  Or a flirting fan attract a man
  To a skirt that shows an ankle!

  For Spain's a land of sun and song,
  Where people flirt the whole day long;
  A state of things that would not be

If the country had to deal with me!

PUCK *and* JELF: Oh, Spain's a land of sun and song,
Where Spaniards flirt the whole day long;
A state of things that wouldn't occur
If they had to flirt all day with *her*!

Exit NELL. *Two Fairies enter. Quartette dance.*

Enter JOY *and* BROOK.

BROOK: Do you want a boat to-day, miss?

JOY: No, thank you, Mr. Green.

BROOK: You know me—in these clothes? Why are *you* dressed like that, Miss Jellicoe?

JOY: We won't talk about what we wear, but what we *are*—total strangers.

BROOK: With pleasure.

JOY: Why did you follow me?

BROOK: I didn't recognize you, being a total stranger. I suppose I happened to get into the same train, and out at the same station. When are you going to be married, Miss Jellicoe? Miss Jellicoe?

JOY: You cannot know my name, being a total stranger.

BROOK: Perhaps you have changed it already, as well as your dress. Do you know why *I* am dressed like this?

JOY: Like a sort of sailor?

BROOK: I cannot expect to be the right sort, for your taste, of course. But all sorts of young ladies worship sailors of *some* sort, don't they?

JOY: Do they?

BROOK: You ought to know.

JOY: Well, I know of one who didn't once; but she was not a young lady—only a servant girl.

BROOK: Perhaps *her* sailor wasn't a prince.

JOY: Perhaps not.

BROOK: A lass that loved a sailor not?

JOY: And a sailor loved, alas!

SONG.—JOY.

He was a simple sailor man.
And she a serving maid;

She wore a dress of humble print
According to her grade.
And on her head a servant's cap
Of muslin (*with a spot*),
But though attracted by a "beau,"
She loved a sailor not!

So when he hired a pleasure boat
To take her for a sail,
She would not leave the dock, because
He could not find the bail!
And, as she could not swim, she said
She'd stick to port (*and buns*),
And take him for a sale instead
At Peter Robinson's.

It was the sort of summer sale
That ladies all prefer;
She said she wanted muslin (but
He could not muzzle her).
And when he paid the bill, said he,
"I feel that put about,
That I'll put out to sea, or she
Will see that I'm put out!"

So Jack went on his ship again,
More wages for to earn;
And though he was a kindly chap
He now did look astern.
"Give me a lock of hair," he cried;
"Choose what you will," said she.
(She knew he could not pick that lock
While she stood on the quay!)

Now, when she'd made that muslin up
In caps extremely smart,
She set them all at someone else
Which broke that sailor's heart!
And to his mates he loudly swore,
In language unrefined,

"Although I felt all right before,
I now feel left behind!"

And ere he died, he gave a hint
To other sailor chaps:
"Don't trust a single thing in print,
Unless set up in caps!
For girls may say that handy-men
Are sweet as sugar-candy;
But that is their opinion when
No other man is handy!"

Exit into Inn.

BROOK: Don't go, Joy! I have something to say to you! Joy! Joy!

JOY (*appearing at upper window*): What is it?

BROOK: Do you really prefer soldiers to sailors?

JOY: I can't tell you now. I'm too busy.

BROOK: How long will you be busy?

JOY: For an hour, I expect.

BROOK: Why, what have you got to do?

JOY: Well, I have to turn out two bedrooms and scrub the floors and clean the windows and dust all the furniture, and then milk the cows and feed the pigs, and chop some wood and lay the kitchen fire, which has gone out, and light it, and peel some potatoes, and shell some peas, and make an apple pie, and make some bread and put it in the oven. And pick some red currants and clean them and make twelve dozen pots of jam, and take all the linen out of the press and look through it, and mend it and put it back again, and darn three pairs of stockings, and catch a fowl and kill it and pluck it and cook it, and clean a pair of boots, and go and change my frock.

BROOK: What will you be doing for the rest of the hour?

JOY: I may not have any rest.

BROOK: During the rest of the hour will you come out here, and let me tell you all that is in my heart.

JOY: No. Go away.

BROOK: Don't send me away. Joy!

JOY: Well?

BROOK: If I talk to you from down here, do you think you will be able to hear me through the open window?

JOY: Perhaps. (*Shuts it*)

BROOK: Very well. If you take that line, I'll take this! (*Military music heard*)

YAPP *enters, preceding the Band of the Royal Marines, Light Infantry.* PUCK *leading them as drum-major.* AZURIEL *plays the big drum, and* KENNA *is dressed as a vivandière. The* RECRUITING SERGEANT *enters with them.*

ENSEMBLE *and* CHORUS.

SERGEANT: It's a pressing invitation that I bring
    To the British population from the King:
    Will you serve him on the dry land,
    Will you serve him on the sea?
    Or a bit of both together,
    Like the likes of me?

YAPP: Have you any inclination for to roam?
    Do you want to be a sticky stay-at-home?
    Do you always want to travel
    In a tube or on a 'bus,

SERGEANT, YAPP, PUCK: Or a battleship or cruiser,
    Like the likes of *us*?

PUCK: Then who'll stand dumb
    When the drum says "Come!"
    If he know what the drum-beat means?
    Don't you be a molly-colly
    Say "Good-bye, Polly,"
    And join the Red Marines!

CHORUS: Then who'll stand dumb, etc.

(*The Band, under* PUCK's *direction, plays the Refrain and manoeuvres across the stage*)

SERGEANT: Do you want to look particularly spruce,
    For ornament, additional to use?
    With a waist of eighteen inches,
    And a chest of forty-three,
    With medals hung upon it
    Like the likes of me?

YAPP: Have you any preparations for to make?
    Any feminine relations to forsake?
    Is there any pretty baggage
    You will leave upon the quay

SERGEANT, YAPP, PUCK: Who can like you any better
  Than my own likes me?
PUCK: Then don't stand dumb
  When the drum says "Come!"
  Now you know what the drum-beat means;
  Don't you be a molly-colly
  Say "Good-bye, Polly,"
  And join the Roy'l Marines!
CHORUS: Then don't stand dumb, etc. (*Business of Band as before*)
SERGEANT: Have you any hesitation in your mind?
  Is there any combination you can find
  Like a dash of Tommy Atkins,
  With a spice of Jolly Tar,
  When you roll 'em both together
  Which is what we are!
YAPP: Do you want to be a Duke of Wellington?
  And a Beresford and Kitchener in one?
  A modern Alexander
  (Not to mention Mr. tree),
SERGEANT, YAPP, PUCK: Or any other hero
  Like the likes of me!
PUCK: Then don't stand dumb
  For the drum says "Come!"
  And you know what the music means
  Don't you be a molly-colly
  Say "Good-bye, Polly,"
  And join the Red Marines!
CHORUS: Then don't stand dumb, etc. (*Band as before*)
Enter BROOK.
BROOK: Sergeant, I'm your man!
SERGEANT: Spoke like a Briton!
KENNA: I am so glad you are coming—if it will make you happy.
BROOK: One moment. To be perfectly plain with you, I have a
  disappointment in love, and I am joining the service in order to escape
  from feminine society. I did not know you employed young women.
SERGEANT: Well, no more did I, till this Drum-Major reported
  himself to me for duty.
PUCK: It is a new idea to encourage recruiting. Besides taking over
  the Marines from the Admiralty, the War Office have decided to

employ young women as well as old in some of their departments. It is one of their most daring reforms.

BROOK: Well, give me a shilling.

SERGEANT: Giving the shilling's out of date—we promise it instead; it's called reserve pay. Now, come and get your things out of store.

BROOK: I am ready. (*Exeunt, the Band playing*)

Enter JELF.

KENNA (*to* JELF): All you have to do now is to persuade your friend Bill to marry Nell. (*Exit*)

JELF: Is that all?—I see. Bill!

Enter BILL BLAKE.

BLAKE: Yes, William.

JELF: Would you like to marry Nell in place of me?

BLAKE: No, William, that I wouldn't.

JELF: Have you seen this subscription list for Nell's wedding present— the money as will be handed over with Nell on her wedding—to her husband, of course. (*He shows slate, on which are written small sums of money amounting to a few shillings*)

BLAKE: It's a deal o' money—leastways, so I should say.

JELF: You'd say right. Can you tell how much it comes to added up?

BLAKE: No, William. I ain't at all handy with figures since I hurt my thumb.

JELF: Couldn't you find out what it comes to with a piece of chalk— not in your head, but figurin' it out with a lump o' chalk?

BLAKE: I don't know how you find that out with a lump of chalk, or a lump of anything else, though I know things *is* shown that way.

JELF: *Things*! There's any amount of things as a handy chap can teach a ignorant with a bit o' chalk. (*Aside*) And a bit o' cheek. Anything, from philosophy to figures.

BLAKE: What's philosophy, William?

JELF: Philosophy? Why knowin' that one woman's better nor two men if she puts her mind to it. Look here.

The proper study of Mankind
(Accordin' to the Pope)
Is Man! Bun Woman we may find
Is proper too, I hope!
Take Man, and take a lump of chalk
And add two letters, so:

They'll teach you more than hours of talk,
That W, and O!

So learn, as quickly as you can,
The lesson they be tellin'—
That Woman's double you, O Man,
In sense, as well as spellin'!

Geography:—here's E, F, G:
You'll recognize, perhaps,
They're England, France, and Germany,
Accordin' to the maps!
And H.M.S. a British ship
A-cruisin' round our coast.
And givin' foreigners the tip—
But there, we mustn't boast!

And these here waves as I've put there
Might be, perhaps, more wavy;
But then we've learned, as you're aware,
To rule 'em, in the Navy!

Arithmetic:—I now engage
To show, as you shall see,
A lady can reduce her age
To what she'd like to be!
Subtract two feet from off her waist—
Divide 'em down below:
And eyes and lips and hair to taste—
And there's a gal I know!

And though her figure, I'll be bound,
Might very well be lanker—
What matter if the figure's round
She's keeping with her banker!

BLAKE: Well, what about that subscription? What does it come to?
JELF: I'd forgotten that.
BLAKE: I hadn't. That's what I've been waitin' for, while you've been talkin'.

EDWARD GERMAN AND BASIL HOOD

JELF (*making a pretence of adding up and putting down the result*): It comes to three thousand pounds and a penny-halfpenny.

BLAKE: Three thousand pounds!

JELF: And a penny-halfpenny!

BLAKE: And Nell.

Enter NELL.

JELF: Yes, she's thrown in.

NELL: What are you saying about me?

JELF: Why, Miss, them gipsies made a mistake. Bill's the prince. And he's ready to marry you instead o' me. (*To* BILL) You know you are!

NELL: The question is, whether I am ready to marry *him*.

JELF: I don't think there'd be no question about that. He's a man.

NELL: Yes; but is he a *bad* one?

JELF: Bad? Bill, just tell the lady that piece of po'try of yours.

BLAKE: There ain't no harm in that.

JELF: Wherever there's any bad language I'll whistle, so as you can stop your ears. Bill's that there bad himself that he don't know bad language when he hears it. Go on, Bill.

BLAKE: "There once was a—(JELF *whistles*)—parrot." There's no bad word there, William. The word's "pretty."

JELF: *You* may think it's pretty, Bill, a lady wouldn't. Go on.

BLAKE: "There was once a pretty parrot,
    As was living wild and free,
    Till some—(*whistle*)—British sailors"
The proper word before "British sailors" is—

JELF: Don't you dare to say the proper word, or that the word is proper, 'cos it ain't.

NELL: What *is* the word?

BLAKE: "Wicked," ma'am.

JELF: There! What did I say?

BLAKE: "Till some wicked British sailors
    Come and knocked him off his tree."
Leave me alone, William!

JELF (*aside*): Why don't you leave *me* alone. It's all for the best. She won't marry you unless.

NELL (*to* JELF): If I do not hear the recitation, I cannot possible judge if it is wicked. Do not whistle any more.

JELF (*to* BILL): I shall have to think of some other proof of your wickedness now. (*To* NELL) Do you know why Blake here is known as "Rainbow Bill," ma'am?

NELL: No!

JELF: It will show he's bad enough for you to marry, ma'am.

BLAKE: What are you goin' to say now?

JELF: A piece of po'try *I* know. (*To* NELL) He's called "Rainbow Bill" by all who knows him, because though *we* know his name's Blake, he's got

A Mrs. Brown in Portsmouth Town,
And at Plymouth a Mrs. Blue;
And a Mrs. Scarlett somewhere else,
And a Mrs. Yaller, too;
And a Mrs. Indigo somewhere's
(*I think she lives at Hove*),
And a Mrs. Green at Rottingdean,
And somewhere's Mrs. Mauve!
So I don't think you need think twice about marryin' *him*, miss—do you?

NELL: No! I thought of it *once*. I must think of it no more. A Mrs. Green at Rottingdean, and a Mrs. Mauve at Hove! Oh! I shall never marry now! Never! Never! (*Exit*)

Enter REDDISH *and* DOUBLEDAY.

REDDISH: *What* did she say?

JELF: That she don't mean to marry—not me, nor any one else. She said I before witnesses. You've took me in about here, that's what you've done. You've buoyed me up with false hopes, that's what you've done. You've broken a honest sailor's heart, that's what you've done. And I've a very good mind to knock you about, only I ain't got time. Come along, Bill. (*Exeunt*)

DOUBLEDAY: W-w-what does it m-m-m-m—

REDDISH: What does it mean? Why, that they've played a game on us, a game of old maid, and we've lost. That's what it means!

BROOK *enters with the* SERGEANT. *He is in uniform. Enter* JOY.

JOY: You must not go!

BROOK: Yes! As the girl I love won't tell me which she prefers—a soldier or a sailor—I'll be both, and join the Marines! As the girl

I love was too busy to listen to me, I listened to the recruiting sergeant.

Joy: No, no! Sergeant, you must not take him!

Sergeant: Too late, miss. He's taking the King's shilling.

Joy: What's one shilling from a sovereign?

Brook: I am ready.

Sergeant: Quick, march!

Joy: No, no! Don't go! I was only teasing you because you were jealous. Don't go! Don't go! (*Exeunt*)

Puck: Now every one is thoroughly happy, except me; and I've had to do most of the work. Butterfly! (*Enter* Butterfly)

Butterfly: Here.

Puck: How like you me in this shape? How do I tickle your taste?

Butterfly: So as to make me laugh.

Puck: Well, I would have your smiles; and a laugh is a smile magnified. So laugh, if you will love me, and I will take any shape that makes you laugh most, fish, flesh or fowl!

Song.—Puck *and* Butterfly.

Puck: Oh, if I were a barn-door fowl,
    And you a barn-door hen,
    Do you suppose that you would scowl
    On my proposals then?
    And if I serenaded you
    According to my wont,
    And I sang "Cock-a-doodle-doo,"
    Would you say "Doodle-don't"?
    Or would you care to fly
    With such a fowl as I?
    Such a worn-to-a-phantomy, love-sick young Bantamy, game little fowl as I?

Both: Such a worn-to-a-phantomy, etc.

Puck: Suppose I were a little sheep,
    And you a lambkin too,
    We'd run away from our Bo-Peep,
    A little ram and ewe;
    For if I boldly said, "Oh, dam"
    (Addressing your mamma),

"Will you give me your little lamb?"
I think she'd answer "Bah";
But would you care to fly
With such a sheep as I—
Such a skippety, hopperty, run-through-his-property, black little
sheep as I?

BOTH: Such a skippety, hopperty, etc.

PUCK: I would I were a little rook,
And you a rook like me,
I'd ask you then to come and look
At our old family tree;
And you and I on marriage bent
Would clasp each others claws,
For there'd be no impediment
(Although, perhaps, some caws);
But would you care to fly
With such a bird as I—
Such a very coal-blackety, rickety, rackety, rascally rook as I?

BOTH: Such a very coal-blackety, etc.

(*the following two verses do not appear in the vocal score*)

PUCK: And if I were a tabby Tom
And you a tabby maid,
Would you enjoy extractment from
My feline serenade?
If I awaked my sleeping mews
Should I awake you too?
And when I sang "Whom do you choose?"
Would you reply, "M'*you*!"
Oh, would you care to fly
With such a cat as I—
Such a mewlity, meowlity, out-on-the-prowlity, Tom on the tiles
as I?

BOTH: Such a mewlity, etc.

PUCK: And if I were a piggy-wig
And you a piggy too,
You would not find a rasher pig
In all I'd promise you;
For at your trotters I would fling
Myself, and there propose!

But would you let me put a ring
Upon your little nose?
Oh would you care to fly
With such a pig as I?
Such a ready-to-die for you, sty-in-my-eye for you, lovesick young
bore as I?

BOTH: Such a ready-to-die for you, etc.

Exeunt.

Enter JOY. *Enter* James JELLICOE *and* YAPP.

JELLICOE: Joy!

JOY: Is it really you, father?

YAPP: Yes, Miss. He's proved it, with the papers in his note-case, to
the satisfaction of the law. I've taken a note of the case. (*Showing
bank-note*)

JELLICOE: Go and stop that young man being taken as a recruit. He is
in my employment, and he cannot enlist without my permission.

YAPP: That's the law, Sir James Jellicoe, sir.

JELLICOE: Then hurry after him.

YAPP: Yes, Sir James. (*Exit*)

JELLICOE: Come with me, my dear.

Enter BEN.

JOY: It all seems like a dream—a Midsummer Day dream. (*Exit with*
JELLICOE)

BEN: Dream! I've just waked up again! Why do they want to have
bands playin' when I'm dreamin'? (*Sleeps under tree*)

(NELL *enters*)

NELL: I have decided to marry Ben. I believe he is even worse than
he looks. I shall tell him as soon as he wakes. I wonder what he is
dreaming of. (*She sits beside him*)

JOY *enters, she sings.* BROOK *joins her.*

FINALE.

JOY *and* BROOK: Seven o'clock in the evening,
    Upon a day in June!
JOY: A thousand throats
    Do pipe glad notes
    And I will join their tune!
BROOK: I'll meet my love

And greet my love,
And sing my love a lay
At seven o'clock in the evening
Upon a summer's day.

Other Principals enter. BLAKE, JELF, WEATHERLY, *and* JOHNSON *enter.*
CHORUS *enter.*

QUARTETTE OF SAILORS: Now maybe we're married men,
And maybe we ain't,
But this here's our characters
Without any paint:
Just four plain bluejackets as
Is fond of a spree
That's Bill Blake, Will Weatherly,
Jem Johnson, and me.

PUCK *enters, with Band.*

PUCK: Now, don't stand glum,
For the drum says "Come!"
(*And you've heard what our music means*)
"Don't you be a molly-colly,
Say 'Good-bye, Polly!'
And join the Red Marines!"

ALL: We won't stand glum, etc.

CHORUS: Sound, sound a Bridal March,
Love hath come again.

KENNA, AZURIEL, *and* CHORUS: Nature, sound thy diapason,
Let thy thousand, thousand voices
Sing in praise of Love triumphant,
For Love hath come again!

CURTAIN

Appendix

Song.—Brook.

My heart a ship at anchor lies
Upon the azure of thine eyes,
Whose rippling glances come and go
To toss my heart from weal to woe.
Oh! If one tear should rise for me,
'Twould be a pearl from that fair sea!
And such a jewel I would prize
Beyond the hope of Paradise!

Then drive my heart, all tempest-tossed,
On that dark shore where souls are lost;
But grudge me not that merchandise,
One little tear from thy sweet eyes!
Yet if my heart lie broken there,
Wrecked by the maelstrom of despair,
The favouring zephyr of thy sighs
May guide it back where haven lies!

A Note About the Author

Edward German (1862–1936) and Basil Hood (1864–1917) were famous British composers and lyricists. German wrote and played music as a child, eventually becoming a teacher at the Royal Academy of Music. Hood started in the British Army, where he initially wrote plays as a hobby. Both men created the bulk of their work during the late nineteenth and early twentieth centuries. Hood wrote *Gentleman Joe, the Hansom Cabbie* (1895), *The French Maid* (1896), and *Little Hans Andersen* (1903). German made a name for himself with *The Two Poets* (1886), *The Rival Poets* (1901) and *Tom Jones* (1907).

A Note from the Publisher

Spanning many genres, from non-fiction essays to literature classics to children's books and lyric poetry, Mint Edition books showcase the master works of our time in a modern new package. The text is freshly typeset, is clean and easy to read, and features a new note about the author in each volume. Many books also include exclusive new introductory material. Every book boasts a striking new cover, which makes it as appropriate for collecting as it is for gift giving. Mint Edition books are only printed when a reader orders them, so natural resources are not wasted. We're proud that our books are never manufactured in excess and exist only in the exact quantity they need to be read and enjoyed.

bookfinity™

Discover more of your favorite classics with Bookfinity™.

- Track your reading with custom book lists.
- Get great book recommendations for your personalized Reader Type.
- Add reviews for your favorite books.
- AND MUCH MORE!

Visit **bookfinity.com** and take the fun Reader Type quiz to get started.

Enjoy our classic and modern companion pairings!

Classic & Modern

www.ingramcontent.com/pod-product-compliance
Lightning Source LLC
Chambersburg PA
CBHW020558030426
42337CB00013B/1132